A COMPANION GUIDE TO ENῑ ˍ..

A COMPANION GUIDE TO ENFORCEMENT

NIGEL STONE

OWEN WELLS PUBLISHER

Published by

Owen Wells Publisher
23 Eaton Road
Ilkley
West Yorkshire
LS29 9PU

Tel (0943) 602270
Fax (0943) 816732

Book production by

Groundwork
Skipton
North Yorkshire

Printed in Great Britain

CONTENTS

REFERENCES

P. Cooper and J. Cooper (1993) 'Duplicity in Informations', *Probation Journal*, 40(4), 199–200.

HM Inspectorate of Probation (1993) *Probation Orders with Requirements for Psychiatric Treatment*, Home Office.

C. Lawson (1978) *The Probation Officer as Prosecutor*, Institute of Criminology, Cambridge University.

R. Ward and S. Ward (1993) *Community Sentences: Law and Practice*, Blackstone Press.

GLOSSARY

ACR	automatic conditional release/Attendance Centre Rules 1958
BA	Bail Act 1976
CJA	Criminal Justice Act
CJPOA	Criminal Justice and Public Order Act 1994
CPS	Crown Prosecution Service
Cr App R(S)	Criminal Appeal Reports (Sentencing)
Crim LR	Criminal Law Review
CSO	community service order
CSCOR	Community Service and Combination Order Rules 1992 (SI 1992/2076)
CYPA	Children and Young Persons Act 1969
DPP	Director of Public Prosecutions
J	Justice of the High Court
LAA	local authority accommodation
LJ	Lord Justice of Appeal
MCA	Magistrates' Courts Act 1980
MCR	Magistrates' Courts Rules 1981
MC(CJA 1991)(MA)R	Magistrates' Courts (CJA 1991) (Miscellaneous Amendments) Rules 1992 (SI 1992/2072)
MC(C&YP)R	Magistrates' Courts (Children and Young Persons) Rules 1992 (SI 1992/2071)
MC(F)R	Magistrates' Courts (Forms) Rules 1981
PACE	Police and Criminal Evidence Act 1984
PCCA	Powers of Criminal Courts Act 1973
PR	Probation Rules 1984 (SI 1984/647)
PSA	petty sessions area
SCA	Supreme Court Act 1981
SI	Statutory Instrument
STO	secure training order
WLR	Weekly Law Reports
YOI	young offender institution

FOREWORD

This Guide tries to provide a reasonably comprehensive outline of the relatively esoteric business of enforcing community orders and allied provisions for statutory supervision of offenders. I am not aware of any comparable work on the market. Most legal practitioners' textbooks do only scant justice to the enforcement of community sentences and are usually too technical or too general to be readily accessible to social workers and probation officers. Court clerks often have a somewhat hazy grasp of the myriad provisions which play a relatively small part in their daily tasks and tend frequently to look to court duty officers to have the answers to unexpected questions.

The mantle of prosecutor still fits somewhat uneasily on the shoulders of probation officers and social workers who may temperamentally align themselves more readily with defence-minded considerations or the neutral role of adviser to sentencers. However, the era described by Colin Lawson in *The Probation Officer as Prosecutor* (1978), when breach proceedings were few and far between, is long gone and though it is not my intention to overstate the place of a sound legal knowledge base, it is nevertheless important for every practitioner to have a working grasp of the legal context in which we supervise and help offenders. This book may serve to boost the reader's confidence and help them both to 'get it right' and to treat offenders fairly and with proper regard to due process of law.

This is obviously not a practice book in the proper sense and so it is not possible to do justice to the scope for sensitive practice and the exercise of discretion in managing statutory responsibilities effectively without reaching for the enforcement button. That is an implicit assumption, in recognition that the individuals caught up in statutory demands are frequently coping with adverse circumstances and would probably not be where they are if their capacity for conformity was as well tuned as the rules sometimes seem to demand. It was, for example, alarming to read in a Probation Inspectorate thematic report (1993) on psychiatric probation orders that:

> 'probationers were being convicted of breach of requirement because they were reacting exactly in accordance with the mental condition diagnosed in the first place to a poorly managed situation'.

It is regrettable that the revised (1994) version of *National Standards for the Supervision of Offenders in the Community* offers little recognition of the need for flexibility 'in the interests of the objectives of the order' and takes instead a rather more rigid line on enforcement decision-taking. It has, however, been possible to draw only on the near final draft of the 1994 edition; the paragraphs cited may therefore change, in numbering at least if not in spirit. I have also assumed that the Criminal Justice and Public Order Bill will receive Royal Assent in its current form.

Working part-time as a magistrates' court liaison probation officer, I am all too aware that there are not neat answers to every problem and that there remains considerable scope for local tradition, variation and canny resort to pragmatic procedural flexibility. Many areas of statutory ambiguity remain, as yet uninterpreted by the Court of Appeal, and in the nature of things are likely to continue so. I certainly do not offer a guarantee that all the answers can be found within these pages, but I hope that the contents do at least provide the best and handiest reference book around without constant recourse to a mobile library of Acts, manuals and law reports. There are bound to be errors and omissions and I would be grateful for the constructive criticism and comments of readers so that these can be rectified in any future editions.

A word about language. I know that the use of the term 'offender' is not an altogether happy label but I have opted to use it throughout to reflect legislation consistently. I have, however, sought wherever possible to correct Parliament's persisting assumption that the offender and enforcer are always male.

Nigel Stone

Norwich, July 1994

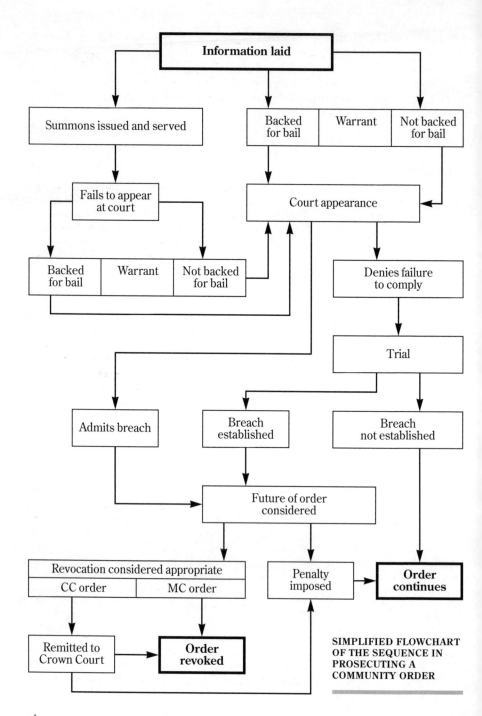

Information laid

Summons issued and served

| Backed for bail | Warrant | Not backed for bail |

Fails to appear at court

| Backed for bail | Warrant | Not backed for bail |

Court appearance

Denies failure to comply

Trial

Admits breach

Breach established

Breach not established

Future of order considered

| Revocation considered appropriate | | Penalty imposed | **Order continues** |
| CC order | MC order |

Remitted to Crown Court

Order revoked

SIMPLIFIED FLOWCHART OF THE SEQUENCE IN PROSECUTING A COMMUNITY ORDER

1.
CONDUCTING A PROSECUTION AND OTHER ENFORCEMENT PROCEEDINGS

This Chapter provides a generic outline of procedure, primarily in the context of breach proceedings.

Laying an Information

Enforcement proceedings alleging a breach of a requirement of a community order (with the exception of a supervision order, see page 23) or YOI supervision or of a condition of short-term prisoner (ACR) licence or of STO supervision are initiated by the 'laying of an information', the key to securing an offender's appearance before the court. An information is simply an allegation that a person has committed either an offence or, more usually in this context, a failure to comply with a requirement, and provides the basis for the issue of a summons or a warrant.

Jurisdiction

Details of the petty sessions area and courts having jurisdiction to deal with enforcement proceedings and thus to receive an information initiating prosecution are outlined in the chapters dealing with specific orders and post-custodial statutory supervision. All proceedings must commence in a magistrates' court, even though the order was imposed by the Crown Court. If the order was made by a youth court or upon an offender who was aged under 18 at the time of sentence, jurisdiction to deal with enforcement proceedings will depend on the age of the offender at the point when enforcement proceedings are commenced. If the offender is now aged 18 or over, the appropriate venue will be the adult court; if the offender is still aged under 18, the appropriate venue will be the youth court.

Who Lays an Information?

An information must be laid by a named individual and thus cannot be in the name of a Probation Service, a Police Force or a Local Authority. A defect of this nature need not nullify proceedings. Thus in *Rubin v DPP* [1990] 2 QB 80, a prosecution for speeding initiated in the name of 'Thames Valley Police' was held to be valid as the defendant could easily have ascertained who the actual prosecutor was by asking the police force concerned and no injustice had been caused. However, it is clearly preferable to get things right by specifying an individual informant who can be the prosecutor in person, their counsel or solicitor or any other authorised person (MCR 1981 r4(1)). Some agencies opt to lay all informations in the name of a Chief Officer rather than the individual employee directly involved, though this is not the prevailing tradition in the Probation Service.

In regard to the community orders regulated in common by CJA 1991 sch 2 (probation orders, community service orders, combination orders and curfew orders), specific statutory recognition is given to 'the responsible officer' for a number of purposes and although this officer is not statutorily required to initiate breach prosecutions it is very likely that this individual will be the appropriate informant. 'Responsible officer' is defined by CJA 1991 s15(3) as follows:

probation order: the probation officer responsible for the offender's supervision;

community service order: the 'relevant officer', *ie* a probation officer assigned to the task or person appointed for the purpose by the Probation Committee (PCCA 1973 s14(4));

combination order: the Act does not assign overall responsibility, treating each element as if it were a probation order or community service order but the *National Standard* specifies that one probation officer should take overall responsibility for the supervision and enforcement of the order;

curfew order: the person responsible for monitoring the offender's whereabouts during curfew periods.

For attendance centre orders, the relevant statute, CJA 1982 s18, recognises the role of 'the officer in charge' who is thus the appropriate person to lay an information or make any application.

What Should the Information Contain?

Happily, the form to be used for an information alleging failure to comply with a requirement of probation, community service or combination order is specified by MC(CJA 1991)(MA)R 1992 sch 2 Form 92I. For an allegation of failure to comply with an attendance centre order, see MC(C&YP)R 1992 sch 2 Form 7. Generally speaking, however, an information should state:

- the name of the informant;

- the informant's work address;

- the name and address of the accused person;

- details of the order, licence or supervision period allegedly contravened, including the court which made the order or custodial sentence, the date and duration of the order or sentence;

- brief particulars of the alleged failure to comply.

An example of the information for breach of CSO, using Form 92I, is provided in this Chapter. Sample informations for breach of ACR licence and YOI supervision are given in the relevant Chapters.

If an information as originally drafted subsequently proves to be incomplete or inaccurate, the prosecution can make application in court to amend and rectify. If the defence then feel that the error has prejudiced their scope to prepare properly, an adjournment should be granted to allow them extra time to consider their position.

Rule against Duplicity

The basic rule is that an information may allege only one offence (or failure to comply): MCR 1981 r12(1). The basis of the rule is one of fairness so that the defendant can enter an appropriate separate plea to each distinct offence or default allegation. This seemingly simple rule is far from straightforward to apply in practice and has proved vexing in a number of appeal cases not related to enforcement proceedings. The issue is 'a matter offact and degree in each case' but the critical question or test appears to be: 'Can the separate acts attributed to the accused fairly be said to form a single activity or transaction or

GREAT BIRCHAM MAGISTRATES COURT

Date :	1 October 1994
To (accused) :	Wayne Ivor HURT **DoB :** 14.2.1973
Address :	439 Poppyfields Way, Great Bircham, Loamshire

Details of Order

Delete as applicable :
~~Probation Order *~~   **Community Service Order ***   ~~Combination Order *~~

Court which made the Order :   Crown Court at Lymeswold

Date of Order : 8.4.1994   **Duration of Order :** 180 hours

Offence in respect of which Order made :   Aggravated Vehicle Taking

Petty Sessions Area specified in Order :   Great Bircham

Information laid by :	Melanie PAYNE, Probation Officer
Address :	Probation Office, Ficklegate, Great Bircham, Loamshire

Who (upon oath) states that the accused has failed to comply with the requirements of the above Order.

Alleged failure to comply with requirement(s) :
On Sunday 8 July 1994, failed to comply with a reasonable work direction issued by the supervisor, by refusing to undertake a task assigned to him at the work site.

Taken (and sworn) before me   Justices' Clerk/
                                               Justice of the Peace

---

Return date information :	Great Bircham Magistrates Court
Court date and time :	on 21 October 1994 at 10.00 am
Delete as applicable :	~~Summons *~~ **Warrant with bail *** ~~Warrant no bail *~~

Information for Breach of Requirements of Probation Order, Community Service or Combination Order several?' The 'single activity' may involve more than one act. The rule 'rests ultimately on common sense and pragmatic considerations of what is fair in all the circumstances' (*Blackstone's Criminal Practice*, 1994 p1140).

None of the reported cases directly address duplicity in the context of probation or social worker prosecutions. The question is most likely to arise where it is alleged that the offender has failed to attend for appointments on a number of dates. The argument has been put by Cooper and Cooper (1993) that if these alleged defaults arise from a single instruction then there is a *single* failure to comply instanced by a number of omissions, whereas if each of the missed appointments occurred in response to separate instructions then these constitute distinct and thus multiple failures. Unfortunately, their argument rests on case law arising from totally different sets of circumstances (such as whether an information alleging the killing of two red deer without a licence, at the same location and within a very short space of time, was duplicitous! Answer: No, it was a single activity) and is not, in my view, persuasive. It seems more persuasive that each failure is a distinct event, irrespective of whether there is one or more instruction.

The simple way to avoid such problems is to ensure that *separate* informations are laid for each allegation. This has knock on consequences, however. For example, if the allegations are admitted or proved, the offender may be exposed to greater liability, *eg* several, cumulative fines rather than a single fine (see page 20). Alternatively it may well be sufficient to allege a single failure to comply, albeit that this is a 'specimen charge' chosen from a number of possible occasions of breach. There is no intrinsic merit in alleging a string of missed appointments or failures to attend provided that the instance chosen is one for which the presecution evidence is clear and strong. If that allegation is admitted or proved, it is then possible to give the full history of the offender's response. The court's powers are essentially the same whether there is a single failure or ten. The only advantage of multiple allegations seems to be that the offender may be able to claim unanticipated 'reasonable excuse' for one or some but is less likely to be able to do so in respect of all the allegations. There may also be merit in alleging more than one failure where the offender is considered to have defaulted in different ways, for example (in the case of a CSO) by failing to work as instructed, by failing to notify change of address and by failing to follow the reasonable instructions of a supervisor.

If an information is 'bad for duplicity', all is not lost. MCR 1981 r12 permits the prosecution to cure a bad information after proceedings have commenced. If the defence spot a duplicitous defect, the court must ask the prosecutor to choose on which allegation the prosecution case will proceed. The other failures will then be struck out and the court proceeds on the basis of the revised information, subject to any adjournment that the defence may seek if it is considered that they would otherwise be unfairly prejudiced. If the prosecutor fails to elect, the information as a whole must be dismissed.

Oral or Written?

An information may be either oral or in writing. An oral information is thus legally adequate to obtain a summons. The information must be 'in writing and substantiated on oath' (MCA 1980 s1(3)) only if a *warrant* is sought for the arrest of the offender. In fact normal good practice will ensure that the information is written, even if not on oath. The main practical advantage of an oral information arises if the offender is before the court, either in enforcement or other proceedings, and the prosecutor acting for the enforcement agency wishes to bring a new, additional or an alternative allegation 'on the spot', perhaps if the initial allegation appears now to be ill-conceived and an alternative allegation is considered more sound. Even then, an information can usually be quickly placed in writing and submitted to the court.

Time Limits

Enforcement proceedings in respect of a community order must commence while the order 'is in force' (CJA 1991 sch 2 for probation, CS, combination and curfew orders; CYPA 1969 s15 for supervision orders). The exception is the attendance centre order; CJA 1982 s19 does not specify that the order should still be current, thought in almost all instances where breach action is considered appropriate, the order will not have been completed.

In respect of breach of post-custody licence or supervision, where CJA 1991 creates a statutory offence, enforcement proceedings are subject to the general time-limit for summary offences that an information must be laid within six months of the alleged offence (MCA 1980 s127). The provisions for breach of secure training order supervision are oddly anomalous, neither specifying that the order must be in force nor creating an offence (see page 100).

Within these time limits, there is an additional expectation of promptness that an information will be laid within a reasonable time. This was demonstrated in *R v Clerk to the Medway Justices ex parte DHSS* (1986) 150 JP 401 where the Divisional Court upheld the clerk's decision not to issue a summons for social security fraud when almost four months had elapsed between the interview which provided the basis for prosecution and the laying of the information. The Department was comfortably within the 12 month time limit specified for this offence but could offer no satisfactory explanation for the delay.

When is the Information Laid?

A written information is laid (and proceedings thus commenced) when it is received at the office of the clerk to the justices. *Stone's Justices Manual* (1994: 1–5793) comments that 'it can sensibly be inferred that any member of the staff in the office authorised to handle incoming post has authority to receive it'. For the purposes of time limits it is sufficient that the information is received, even if it is not considered by a magistrate or justices' clerk until later (*R v Manchester Stipendiary Magistrate ex parte Hill* [1983] 1 AC 328).

Multiple Orders

An offender may be subject to more than one community order, either because a number of orders were imposed simultaneously for various offences or because different orders have been imposed on separate sentencing occasions, perhaps by different courts. Thus an offender subject to a probation order may subsequently receive a further probation order which overlaps with the initial order where that prior order has not been revoked. Alternatively an offender subject to a community service order may receive a subsequent number of hours to be worked consecutively to the preceding order.

In so far as these considerations affect the initiation of prosecution, the responsible officer should prepare a separate information for each date or sentencing occasion, so that if, for example, four probation orders were imposed on one sentencing occasion, it will only be necessary to lay one information in respect of an alleged failure to comply. If, however, a probation order was imposed by the Crown Court and subsequently a further overlapping probation order is made by a magistrates' court, two informations should be laid in respect of the alleged failure to comply, one in respect of each order.

Where an offender is subject to community service orders imposed on different sentencing occasions and a breach is alleged while the first order remains uncompleted, it is not open to the offender to claim that s/he is in breach only of the first order, on the grounds that the time has not yet arrived to commence the second order. So held the Court of Appeal in *R v Meredith* [1994] Crim LR 142, where the offender had been sentenced to 80 hours CSO by a magistrates' court and a further 160 hours by the Crown Court. Discussing the offender's claim that, as he had completed only 14 hours, he was not in breach of the second order, the Court stated that, if this interpretation were correct, it would 'lead to the remarkable result that he could never be in breach of the second order, because the time would never arrive for him to start performing that order'. The Court added:

> 'Once two community service orders are made they are for all practical purposes one order and he was in breach of both'.

It is thus valid to allege breach of both orders in such instances but two informations should be laid in respect of the alleged failure to comply. If, however, the hours specified in the prior order have been completed, then the alleged breach is in respect of the latter order only and thus only one information will be appropriate. The overall issue of the court's jurisdiction to deal with orders imposed separately on an offender by courts of different levels is complex and is addressed further in Chapter 8.

Issue of Process

A justice before whom an information is laid has power either: (i) to issue a summons directing the offender to appear before a magistrates' court acting for that petty sessional area, or (ii) to issue a warrant to arrest that person and bring him or her before the court. In the case of community orders regulated in common by CJA 1991 sch 2, the power is contained in paragraph 2:

> (1) If at any time while a relevant order is in force in respect of an offender it appears on information to a justice of the peace acting for the petty sessions area concerned that the offender has failed to comply with any of the requirements of the order, the justice may:
>
> (a)　issue a summons requiring the offender to appear at the place and time specified in it; or
>
> (b)　if the information is in writing and on oath, issue a warrant for his arrest.
>
> (2) Any summons or warrant issued under this paragraph shall direct the offender to appear or be brought before a magistrates' court acting for the petty sessions area concerned.

In the case of attendance centre orders, the equivalent power is continued in CJA 1982 s19(1) (see Chapter 6); for secure training orders, CJPOA 1994 s4(1) (see Chapter 12). In the case of ACR Licence and YOI supervision, the power is given by the general provisions of MCA 1980 s1(1).

Though it is formally a matter of discretion, a magistrate should not issue a warrant for arrest if a summons would appear to offer an effective means of securing the offender's attendance before the court. Thus the responsible officer will normally seek a summons in the first instance unless the offender's present whereabouts are unknown, making the service of a summons of doubtful effectiveness.

Issue of Summons

Issuing a summons is a judicial exercise and not merely an administrative task. For enforcement purposes, this means that the issuer of the summons must be satisfied that: (a) the information alleges an offence or failure to comply that is 'known to the law'; (b) it is laid within any applicable time limit; (c) the court has jurisdiction over the matter. If these criteria are satisfied, the summons will almost certainly be issued as it is not necessary for the issuer to consider the prosecution's evidence. Power to issue summons has been extended to justices' clerks but not to their assistants. A summons must be signed by the person issuing it or, in the case of a justice, may state the JP's name authenticated by the clerk's signature. A rubber stamped signature will suffice.

A summons states the substance of the information laid against the offender and the date, time and place at which he or she is required to attend to answer the complaint. A single summons may be issued against a person in respect of several informations but the summons must state the matter of each information separately (MCR 1981 r98(3)).

Summons: Practice Procedure

Practice is often dictated by local conventions and set routine but a typical procedural route to be followed by the responsible officer is as follows:

(i)   Contact the 'listings' section at the justices' clerk's office to arrange a suitable date for a hearing, to be entered on the prospective summons.

(ii)   Send two copies of each information (if more than one allegation is made), retaining a copy on file, together with three copies of the prospective summons to the justices' clerk. It is helpful though not essential to attach a photocopy of the relevant order or licence.

(iii)   Await the consideration and signing of the information (one copy of which is retained by the court) and the return of the three copies of the signed and issued summons.

(iv)   Serve one copy of the summons on the offender, by one of the means outlined below.

Alternatively, the responsible officer (or the court duty officer on their behalf) may lay the information on oath in court before a justice and present the prospective summons, so that the procedure is concertinaed into a single transaction. This ensures that, if subsequently a warrant is sought, there is no need to substantiate the information on oath (see page 11).

In addition, the officer responsible for a community order should notify the prosecution agency which prosecuted the offence(s) for which the order was imposed of the pending breach proceedings so that a file can be available at the court hearing if the order is revoked and details of the original offence are required (see page 21).

Service of Summons

A summons may be served by a choice of means specified by MCR 1981 r99(1), either:

(a)   by personal delivery to the person named, or

(b)   by leaving for that person with some person at their last known or usual place or abode, or

(c)   by sending it by post addressed to that person at their last known or usual place of abode.

Note that for service by post, the usual means of service, it is not necessary for the summons to be sent by registered post or recorded delivery service. The old rule that a summons by post had to be achieved by either of those two means for the court to be satisfied that it was properly served, in the event that the summoned person failed to appear, has been repealed. *Certificate of Service* should be completed by the appropriate employee on the reverse of one of the retained copies of the summons, an appropriate wording being:

I, (name), of (enforcement agency), do hereby certify that I served the addressee overleaf with this document, of which this is a true copy, by:

(sending the said document by post to him/her in a pre-paid letter posted by me on (date) and addressed to him/her at his/her last known or usual place of abode)

or (delivering it personally to him/her on (date)

(Signed and dated)

In some areas the local practice may be for service to be undertaken by the the office of the clerk to the justices rather than by the prosecuting agency.

Warrant for Arrest in the First Instance

A justice before whom an information is laid who has power to issue a summons may alternatively issue a warrant for the arrest of the person named in the summons provided that the information is in writing and substantiated on oath. This power can only be exercised by a magistrate because a clerk is not authorised to take informations on oath.

So far as community sentences are concerned, the statutory provisions governing every community order authorise the issue of a warrant where a failure to comply is alleged. If the default constitutes a criminal offence in its own right then a restriction is imposed by MCA 1980 s1(4) in respect of a person who has attained the age of 18. In this instance a warrant cannot be issued unless either: (i) the offence is indictable or punishable with imprisonment, or (ii) the person's address is not sufficiently established for a summons to be served. This restriction will cause no practical problem because an offence under CJA 1991 s65(6) (failure to comply with YOI supervision) is imprisonable, albeit only a summary offence, and in the prosecution of an offence under CJA 1991 s38(1) (breach of ACR licence conditions), which is not imprisonable, a warrant will not be appropriate unless the offender's whereabouts are unknown. MCA 1980 s1(4) explicitly indicates that the restriction does not apply to youths but a magistrate is likely to apply that restriction as a matter of discretion in cases where the offender is a youth. This issue is most likely to arise in a prosecution for failure to comply with YOI supervision requirements (s 65(6)).

A magistrate issuing a warrant for arrest has the discretion to 'back it for bail', *ie* a direction that the person arrested shall thereafter be bailed by the police to attend court. Such attendance will normally be upon the date specified in the warrant, fixed by the court at the time of issue. This is not essential, however, and in cases where the police may experience difficulty or delay in executing the warrant it may seem sensible for the warrant to specify that the offender shall be bailed to appear before the court on the first convienient date after their arrest, as determined by the police. Local convention may hold that the court's timetable should be determined by the court rather than by the police and that, if the offender's whereabouts are unknown in enforcement proceedings, the warrant should not be backed for bail. In that case the practical choice may thus be between a summons and a warrant not backed for trial but the prosecutor may be reluctant to be instrumental in causing an individual's arrest and detention (possibly overnight), unless the circumstances make this strictly necessary.

Warrant: Practice Procedure

The procedural route to be followed by the responsible officer is as follows:

(i) If in the unusual instance that a warrant backed for bail is sought, the listings officer or section at the justices' clerk's office should be contacted to arrange a suitable date for a hearing, to be entered on the draft warrant.

(ii) Prepare two copies of each information (if more than one allegation is made) and one copy of the draft warrant. It is helpful though not essential to attach a photocopy of the relevant order or licence.

(iii) If the local court procedure practice is to designate a special court consisting of a single justice sitting to deal with applications of this nature, it may be appropriate to contact the listings section to indicate an intention to make the application at the next sitting. It may be more expeditious to bring the matter before a court or justice at any convenient moment during the court's normal sitting day, by arrangement with the court clerk. The local convention is sometimes to provide such an opportunity prior to the start of the court's list.

(iv) In making the application, the responsible officer or the court duty officer on their behalf will: (a) pass the information and warrant to the clerk; (b) enter the witness box and take the oath or affirm, stating their name and role; (c) briefly state the nature of the order or licence to which the offender is subject, the basis of the allegation against the offender, the reason why a warrant is sought and indicate whether the application is for a warrant backed or not backed for bail. There is no exact formula of words to be followed but the necessary information may be conveyed succinctly along the following lines:

> (after the oath or affirmation) 'I am Susan Carter, probation officer with Borsetshire Probation Service, based at Borchester. I am (acting on behalf of Philip Archer, the supervising officer) responsible for the supervision of the probation order made by Ambridge Magistrates on 25 July 1994 in respect of Edward Grundy, for a period of 12 months and which is currently in force, supervised by this court. I am seeking a warrant for the arrest of Mr Grundy as I believe that he has breached that order by moving from his last known address at 25 Church Lane, Borchester in October 1994 without informing (me) (the supervising officer) of his new address and we are unaware of his current whereabouts. In the circumstances a warrant not backed for bail would seem appropriate'.

If the warrant is to be backed for bail, a date will now be fixed for the offender's court appearance, convenient for the prosecutor and the court and allowing sufficient time for the warrant to be executed.

(v)   If the warrant is issued, this will be retained by the clerk to be passed to the police who are responsible for executing it. If it is backed for bail, the person will be called on or other efforts will be made to locate their whereabouts so that he or she may be formally arrested and then released on bail to attend court on the date specified. If the warrant is not backed for bail, the existence of the warrant is normally circulated via the police national computer, so that if the person comes to police attention in any part of the country, they can be detained and brought before the court forthwith. If they are arrested in another part of the country, arrangements for their transport have to be agreed between the police at the point of arrest and the police force serving the issuing court.

(vi)   There may thus be a considerable delay before the person subject to a warrant not backed for bail appears before the court and little scope for anticipating when the matter will surface. When the person is arrested, the prosecuting agency has to be ready to deal with the matter at very short notice, including in the first instance the question of bail, if it is not possible to deal immediately with the substantive breach issue.

The Hearing

If the Offender Answers to Summons: Adjournment

Whether progress can be made at the first hearing will depend on whether the defence is ready to proceed or not. An accused person cannot require an adjournment as of right but is entitled to expect a reasonable opportunity to prepare adequately to answer the accusation and to take legal advice if so desired. It is commonly the case that the offender will not yet have contacted a solicitor or may do so only on the occasion of the court hearing, perhaps approaching the duty solicitor available at the court. Part of the constructive role of the court duty officer may well be to speak to the offender before the hearing and advise them of the desirability of taking legal advice. In such instances the offender's legal representative may well request an adjournment. Power of adjournment may be exercised by a single justice, or by the clerk in the case of a simple adjournment.

On adjourning the case, the court has power to remand the offender, *ie* to commit to custody or to remand on bail, but magistrates have the discretion at this stage simply to adjourn without remand. If the offender has answered to summons, the defence will almost certainly expect a simple adjournment without remand. Normally, a date and time are fixed for the next hearing at the time of adjournment without remand, although this is not an absolute requirement as this can be determined later by the court and notified to the offender (MCA 1980 s10(2)). The court will normally send the offender a notice of adjournment advising of the next hearing date. If the court does opt to remand, a date for the next hearing must be fixed at the time of adjournment.

If the offender fails to reappear following simple adjournment, this does not constitute an offence as it would if they had failed to answer to bail, but it provides an obvious basis for an application for a warrant to be issued for their arrest.

Failure to Answer to Summons

If the offender fails to appear in answer to summons, the court may issue a warrant for the offender's arrest, provided:

(a)   the information has been substantiated on oath, and

(b)   service of the summons is proved, and

(c)   the summons was served a reasonable time before the hearing.

In the case of community orders regulated by CJA 1991 sch 2, this power is provided by sch 2 para. 2 (see page 6); for attendance centre orders, CJA 1982 S19(1); for secure training orders, CJPOA 1994 s4(1). In the case of YOI supervision, power is provided by the general provisions of MCA 1980 s13:

(1) Subject to the provisions of this section, where the court, instead of proceeding in the absence of the accused, adjourns or further adjourns the trial, the court may, if the information has been substantiated on oath, issue a warrant for his arrest.

(2) Where a summons has been issued, the court shall not issue a warrant under this section unless either it is proved to the satisfaction of the court, on oath or in such other manner as may be prescribed, that the summons was served on the accused within what appears to the court to be a reasonable time before the trial or adjourned trial or the accused has appeared on a previous occasion in answer to the information.

(3) A warrant for the arrest of any person who has attained the age of 18 years shall not be issued under this section unless:

(a)   the offence to which the warrant relates is punishable with imprisonment; or

(b)   [not relevant in enforcement proceedings].

If the information was not initially issued on the basis of a sworn information, the information shall now be substantiated on oath by the prosecutor or their appropriate representative such as the court duty officer. This can be covered succinctly along the lines of the following example:

(after the oath or affirmation) 'I am Susan Carter, probation officer with Borsetshire Probation Service, based at Borchester. I am (acting on behalf of Philip Archer, the supervising officer) responsible for the supervision of the probation order made by Ambridge Magistrates on 25 July 1994 in respect of Edward Grundy for a period of 12 months and which is currently in force, supervised by this court. It is alleged that Mr Grundy is in breach of his order by failing to keep an appointment on 16 September 1994, as instructed. I am satisfied that the summons issued on (date) was properly served by a first class letter sent to his last known address at 25 Church Lane, Borchester on 1 October 1994. As he has failed to answer to that summons, I apply for a warrant for Mr Grundy's arrest'.

At this point the question of whether the warrant should be backed for bail or not will arise. This is a matter for the court but the prosecutor is able to express a view. If the offender is believed to be residing at their usual known address then the court is likely to be considering a warrant with bail at this stage, unless the prosecutor wishes to draw its attention to factors which may make such a course seem unproductive. Thus the prosecutor may go on to state:

'As Mr Grundy to the best of the Probation Service's knowledge has a fixed and stable address, a warrant backed for bail would seem appropriate in this instance'.

If the court agrees, the next question to be resolved is the date to be fixed for the next hearing. This will depend largely on the time scale within which the warrants office and the police can be expected to execute the warrant and this is likely to require a minimum of two weeks. A period of between two and six weeks is usual. The prosecutor may have a view of the desirable time scale if he or she wishes to be present at the next hearing and holiday or leave is planned.

Alternatively, the prosecutor may wish to state pertinent information along these lines:

'As the Probation Service's efforts to visit Mr Grundy at this last known address have been unsuccessful and we are informed by a person living there that he is no longer at that address and we are unaware of his present whereabouts, a warrant not backed for bail would seem appropriate in this instance'.

This might well be an appropriate request if the summons posted to the offender's address has been returned by the Post Office marked 'gone away' and this information should certainly be drawn to the court's attention.

Prosecution of an offender for breach of ACR licence under CJA 1991 s38 presents an exception to proceeding under MCA 1980 s13 powers where prosecution is commenced by way of summons, because the breach constitutes a non-imprisonable summary offence and is thus exempted under s13(3)(a). In this special instance, the court may proceed in the offender's absence under MCA 1980 s11(1). This is outlined more fully in Chapter 9 dealing with this form of prosecution.

Failure to Appear following a Warrant backed for Bail

If an offender has been bailed to appear at court following issue of a warrant backed for bail, the court will first wish to know whether the warrant has been executed or not. The prosecutor or the court duty officer will thus need to check this with the warrants office who will be able to indicate whether the police have had the opportunity yet to execute the warrant, whether efforts are still in progress or whether efforts have proved unsuccessful.

If the warrant has been properly executed, the court has the power to issue a warrant for the offender's arrest under the Bail Act 1976 s7. The court has the discretion as before to back the warrant for bail or not. As an alternative to issuing a warrant, the court may adjourn and enlarge the offender's bail in their absence for a further period to a specified later time under MCA 1980 s129(1) or (3)(a). Section 129(1) applies if the court is satisfied that the offender is unable to attend 'by reason of illness or accident'. Section 129(3)(a) applies more broadly and covers circumstances where the offender fails to appear but a reasonable explanation for non-appearance can be given to the court. A solicitor acting for the offender may well be in a position to give an explanation, as may the prosecutor who may be aware of legitimate factors in the offender's current circumstances which have inhibited their attendance. Section 129(3)(a) also conveniently covers instances where the warrant has not been executed because of lack of police time.

If the warrant has not been executed because it has proved impossible to trace the offender, the court has the option to re-issue the warrant for their arrest, this time not backed for bail, as this would have been an option available to the court at the time when the warrant was issued.

If the warrant has not been executed because the police have not yet had the opportunity to seek the offender, the warrant will need to be re-dated, allowing whatever interval appears necessary to give this opportunity.

MCA 1980 s129

(1) If a magistrates' court is satisfied that any person who has been remanded is unable by reason of illness or accident to appear or be brought before the court at the expiration of the period for which he was remanded, the court may, in his absence, remand him for a further time...

(3) Where a person remanded on bail is bound to appear before a magistrates' court at any time and the court has no power to remand him under subsection (1) above, the court may in his absence:

(a) where he was granted bail in criminal proceedings, appoint a later time as the time at which he is to appear and enlarge the recognisances of any sureties for him to that time;

(b) [concerns bail in non-criminal proceedings];

and the appointment of the time... shall be deemed to be a further remand.

Withdrawal of Allegation

Prior to a plea being entered, the prosecution can seek the court's leave to withdraw an allegation. This possibility may well arise if the defence has indicated that it is prepared to admit only one or some of the allegations contained in the informations laid. The prosecution may feel that there is little to be gained by pursuing the contested allegation(s) if, say, the offender is subject to a community order and revocation is sought, the matters which are to be admitted being sufficient to enable the court to exercise its powers of revocation or remittal to Crown Court. Similarly, if breach action has secured the offender's re-engaged compliance with a community order, there may seem little merit in prosecuting the full set of allegations to contested trial. Again, if the offender has now completed their order, the prosecution may feel that there is no advantage in continuing proceedings. If the allegation is withdrawn, this is not equivalent to a finding that the allegation is not proved or, in the case of an offence under CJA 1991 s38 or s65, an acquittal. Consequently, the allegation could be freshly pursued at a later date (subject to the order remaining in force), though this would seem a very unlikely possibility in practice. The offender is not required to be present when leave is sought to withdraw.

Delay and Abuse of Process

Even if proceedings have been initiated within proper time limits, a court has discretion to stop a prosecution when it deems it to be an abuse of the process of the court. This primarily arises at the defence's request where delay arising either inadvertently through inefficiency or otherwise causes prejudice to the defence case. However, there is a clear, general expectation that prosecutions will be proceeded with within a reasonable time. Even if the defence do not object to the slowed pace of the prosecution, the court may raise an objection if the use of process appears designed to prolong proceedings inappropriately. Thus if the prosecution and defence agree that it would be helpful to adjourn proceedings before any plea has been entered to allow the offender an opportunity to re-engage with the relevant order or licence, with the possibility that the prosecution may not proceed if the offender responds satisfactorily, the court may object that this is misuse of court proceedings to pursue an ulterior agenda, with the prosecution simply keeping its options open. The natural wish of the court to 'make progress' can mean that the offender may be encouraged to enter a denial at an early stage, if there appears to be some basis for contesting proceedings, rather than simply allowing matters to stand adjourned without 'progress'. As the case will then probably be adjourned to a date when a contested trial occasion can be fixed (see 'Contested Trial', below), there will still be sufficient opportunity for the offender to re-engage or for defence inquiries to proceed.

Plea

When the offender is present and it is possible to make progress, the next step is to read the information to the offender and ask him or her if, in the case of an allegation of failure to comply, s/he admits or denies the allegation or, in the case of an offence under CJA 1991 s38 or s65, whether s/he pleads guilty or not guilty.

In *R v Devine* [1956] 1 WLR 236, the Court of Appeal gave the following Practice Note directions on the procedure to be adopted in breach of probation order proceedings, applicable in respect of other community orders:

> '...the breach should be put to him in the clearest possible terms and he should be asked to say whether he admits it or not. The way in which it should be put to him is as follows: he should be told the court at which he was convicted; the offence of which he was convicted and the terms of the probation order. He should then be told the grounds upon which it is alleged that he has broken the terms of the probation order... If he admits the matters put to him, the court can then proceed to deal with him. If he denies those matters they must be proved and... the defendant must be asked if he desires to give evidence and call witnesses. After all the evidence has been heard the court must pronounce whether it finds the breach proved. It is, therefore, desirable that the proceedings should begin by the matter being put clearly to the defendant and for him to be asked whether he admits the allegation.'

If the offender admits the allegation or pleads guilty to the offence, it is necessary that the plea should be clearcut and unequivocal. If the offender appears to be qualifying their admission in such a way that suggests a defence (which in this context is likely to be an indication that they have a reasonable excuse for their alleged default) the court must not proceed on the basis of the admission but must attempt to resolve the ambiguity. If the offender's admission remains equivocal the court cannot accept it but will almost certainly give the offender the opportunity to consult their solicitor or to speak to the duty defence solicitor.

Plea by Advocate on Offender's Behalf If the offender answers simply to summons, either at first hearing or following adjournment and is not bailed to appear, it is possible for the offender's advocate to enter a plea on their behalf, certainly a plea of 'denial' to be followed by contested trial at a later date. *Stone's Justices Manual* (1994, para. 1–461) is of the opinion that any plea can be entered by an advocate in a summary trial but offers no authority for this view which seems at odds with the view of the Court of Appeal in *R v Williams* [1978] QB 373 that 'no deviation from the rule that a plea of guilty must come from him who acknowledges guilt is... permissible'. As the court will not proceed to deal with the breach in the offender's absence (with the limited exception of breach of ACR licence: see page 90), this issue is unlikely to be of practical significance.

Change of Plea An offender may change plea from one of admission or guilty to denial or not guilty at any stage before the court deals with the breach or passes sentence, at the court's discretion. Merely because the offender was not legally represented when the original plea was entered does not provide an automatic right to withdraw that plea but is likely to carry persuasive weight with the court.

Uncontested Proceedings

If the offender admits the breach or pleads guilty, the prosecution proceeds essentially in the same manner as follows a plea of guilty in other criminal proceedings, with the prosecutor outlining or summarising the facts. These will usually not be particularly complex, for example if the offender has failed to keep an appointment or to attend for community service work as instructed, but there may be a need for greater elaboration in instances where the offender changed address without notifying the responsible officer or the offender failed to comply with the rules of the hostel or with the instructions of a CS supervisor or with instructions regarding the avoidance of language or behaviour likely to cause serious offence to another. What is different in respect of enforcement prosecutions is that the prosecutor departs from the normal rule that the prosecution does not play an active part in the consideration of sentence and can offer advice and opinion to the court in helping it decide what action to take. This double role is addressed further on page 18.

Contested Trial

If the offender enters a denial or not guilty plea and the prosecution proposes to proceed with the prosecution, the matter is unlikely to proceed straightaway because witnesses are almost certainly not in attendance and the court will wish to adjourn to a date and time when there is adequate space for the trial to be accommodated. Commonly, the matter will be adjourned in the first instance to an intermediate date (to a 'fixing court') when the actual trial date can be fixed in the light of inquiries about witness availability or the availability of evidence that the defence may wish to obtain, and the convenience of the advocates for both the prosecution and the defence. The prosecutor will probably wish to arrange legal representation. Local practice will determine the arrangements for such representation, *eg* using the services of a local authority's legal services department or instructing the firm of solicitors who regularly undertake that work on the agency's behalf.

Offering No Evidence

Once the offender has entered a denial or a not guilty plea to the information, the prosecutor no longer has the option to seek to withdraw the allegation. If it is not considered to be in the interests of justice to pursue the contested matter, for such reasons as outlined in respect of a withdrawal of an allegation, the alternative is to offer no evidence and invite the court to dismiss the allegation. The dismissal of an information prevents the allegation being the subject of a fresh prosecution at a later stage.

What Has to be Established

For a prosecution to be pursued successfully, the prosecutor has to be able to establish the following:

(a) The order or custodial sentence was imposed. This is not likely to be challenged but can, where necessary, be proved by a copy of the order backed, if need be, by obtaining a certi-

fied copy of the appropriate entry in the court register. PACE 1984 s73 provides that a conviction in the United Kingdom may be proved by a certificate of conviction and proving that the person named in the certificate as having been convicted of the offence is the person whose conviction is to be proved. MCR 1981 r68 provides that the register of a magistrates' court or any document purporting to be an extract from the register, certified by the clerk as a true extract, shall be admissible in any legal proceedings as evidence of proceedings of the court entered in the register. SCA 1981 s132 states that 'every document purporting to be sealed or stamped with the seal or stamp of the Supreme Court shall be received in evidence in all parts of the United Kingdom without further proof'.

(b) In the case of licence, notice of YOI supervision or STO supervision, that the offender was released on licence or notice of supervision. This too is unlikely to be challenged but can be established, if necessary, without the direct oral evidence of the governor of the releasing establishment, by tendering evidence of the licence or notice, citing CJA 1988 s24 which permits a statement in a document to be admissible in criminal proceedings as evidence of any fact in respect of which direct oral evidence would be admissible, where 'the document was created by a person... as the holder of a paid... office'.

(c) The offender is the person subject to the order, licence or notice. This too is likely to be admitted without dispute. Proof can be obtained where necessary by evidence of the supervising officer who served a copy of the order upon the offender or conducted an induction interview with the licensee or supervisee upon their release from custody. In the event that the offender was not interviewed by the prosecuting agency prior to initiation of breach proceedings, resort may ultimately be made to the admission of finger print evidence under CJA 1948 s39.

(d) In the case of a community order (other than an attendance centre order, see page 71), *that the order was in force when enforcement proceedings commenced.* It does not matter that the order has since terminated by time expiry or even that the offender has completed their order requirements in the interim. This was established in *R v Tebbutt* (1988) 10 Cr App R(S) 88 where breach proceedings were commenced when 27 hours of a 100 hour order remained outstanding. The matter was remitted to the Crown Court and the offender completed his outstanding hours while waiting to appear there. He subsequently claimed that the order no longer existed and thus the Crown Court had no power to revoke the order and deal with him in another way. The Court of Appeal was not persuaded, declaring that this would have the remarkable effect of handing over control to the offender who:

'would be enabled to wait until breach proceedings have been instituted and then be permitted to elect... to complete the hours... and so escape the risks involved of being dealt with for his original offence'.

(e) The offender is in breach of the order, licence or notice by reason of his or her failure to comply with one or more requirements contained in that order, licence or notice. It is in this respect that the grounds of prosecution are likely to be in contention, on the basis that the instruction giving effect to the requirement:

(i)   was not given; or

(ii)   was not received; or

(iii)   was unreasonable; or

(iv)   was too vague or unclear; or

(v)   was beyond the legitimate authority of the requirement.

Alternatively, the defence may claim:

(vi)   the instruction was complied with; or

(vii)   there was reasonable excuse for the failure to comply; or

(viii)   in the case of a probation or supervision order, the requirement was not lawful because it was too imprecise or accorded undue discretion to the responsible officer.

Such defence claims are considered in more detail in the following Chapters.

The majority of enforcement provisions specifically exclude liability if the offender has reasonable excuse for the failure to comply but, in those instances where this is not specified (*eg* breach of ACR licence), it is suggested that it remains equally open to the offender to make such a claim in their defence.

Burden of Proof

The burden and the standard of proof are exactly as in any other criminal proceedings. The prosecution has the burden of proof to prove the elements of the breach, including the giving of the instruction and the validity of that instruction, beyond reasonable doubt. However, in regard to whether the offender had 'reasonable excuse', it is not for the prosecution specifically to prove the absence of reasonable excuse but for the defence to raise evidence of this, *eg* on grounds of ill-health, family commitments, work demands, etc, being matters within the particular knowledge of the offender. CJA 1991 sch 2 and other statutory enforcement provisions do not specifically place any burden of proof upon the defence and so it is necessary to refer to the general provision of MCA 1980 s101:

Where the defendant to an information or complaint relies for his defence on any exception, exemption, proviso, excuse or qualification, whether or not it accompanies the description of the offence or matter of complaint in the enactment creating the offence or on which the complaint is founded, the burden of proving the exception, exemption, proviso, excuse or qualification shall be on him; and this notwithstanding that the information or complaint contains an allegation negativing the exception, exemption, proviso, excuse or qualification.

The offender has to prove such excuse 'on a balance of probabilities', *ie* 'if the evidence is such that the court can say: "We think it more probable than not", the burden is discharged but, if the probabilities are equal, it is not'.

Note that although *National Standards* or local codes of practice may specify how matters such as ill-health or work commitments should be dealt with, *eg* by requiring a medical certificate or proof from the employer, these are not decisive and the offender is entitled to raise the possibility of reasonable excuse and the court to find such excuse established even though the *Standard* or code of practice has not been complied with.

Producing Evidence

In many instances the presentation of the prosecution case is entirely straightforward, reliant only on the evidence of the responsible officer, *eg* if the alleged failure to comply concerns the offender's non-appearance for interview or work, contrary to an instruction given. In more complex cases the prosecutor is almost certain to obtain legal representation and thus to receive competent advice on the preparation of the case, the admissibility of evidence and the use that may be made of agency records. Statutory provisions concerning the admissibility of documentary evidence, particularly where the potential witness has now left the employ of the prosecuting agency and may be unavailable to attend court without severe inconvenience, under CJA 1988 ss23–26 are complex and cannot be dealt with adequately in this text.

'Newton' Trial

If the offender admits failure to comply, there may nevertheless be a material basis of dispute about the facts of the breach. This is likely to arise only very rarely but may be an issue if, say, in the case of an offender subject to CSO who is said to have issued threats to a work supervisor, the nature of the threats or perhaps the use of a weapon in making those threats may be of significance if the offender is seeking to persuade the court that the order should be allowed to continue. It may thus be necessary for the court to hear evidence by holding a *Newton* hearing, so called after the case which introduced this possibility. It is the responsibility of the defence to notify the prosecution that an admission will be made which disputes the prosecution account. The initiative to hold a Newton hearing lies with the court and is not dependent on either the prosecution or the defence seeking such an inquiry. If the court does not hear evidence, it must normally accept the offender's version of events unless the offender's account is 'so manifestly false', 'untenable' or 'incredible' that the court is entitled to reject it.

The Prosecutor's Failure to Appear

In the unlikely event that the prosecutor does not appear for the trial of an information and the offender is present and seeking to proceed, the court has the discretion under MCA 1980 s15(1) either to dismiss the information or to adjourn the trial. Power to dismiss should not be exercised punitively and should not, for example, be exercised when the magistrates know that the prosecutor is on the way to court and the case is otherwise ready to be presented (*R v Hendon Justices, ex parte DPP* [1993] 2 WLR 862). See also *R v Parker and Barnet Magistrates' Court ex parte DPP* (1994) 158 JP 389 where the prosecution was misinformed by a court officer about the starting time of a trial; the Divisional Court held that it was perverse for the magistrates to refuse an adjournment and to disadvantage the prosecution on the basis of a mistake.

The Role of the Probation Officer or Social Worker if Breach is Established

Once a breach has been established and the court next has to consider what action to take, the probation officer or social worker is in effect required to switch role from that of prosecutor to assisting the court by advising, for example, on the offender's suitability for the order to continue. The tension between these roles are obvious. The legitimate compatibility of these functions was challenged by the offender in *R v Liverpool Magistrates' Court ex parte Atkinson* (1987) 9 Cr App R(S) 216. The probation officer had successfully prosecuted the offender for breach of community service and subsequently invited the court to revoke the order, drawing attention to other instances of alleged breach behaviour which had not been the subject of proceedings. The offender sought judicial review, claiming that the prosecuting officer should not have contributed to the court's decision-making following proof of breach. The court dismissed this argument, Woolf LJ stating:

'...in relation to establishing the matters which it is necessary to establish so that the justices can exercise their powers, in practice the probation officer performs a function very similar to a prosecutor. However, once the breach of the requirement has been established, the magistrates will have an option as to what particular course to adopt and, as with any other court who is responsible for deciding how to deal with an offender, it will require the assistance of the probation officer. Speaking for myself, I can see no objection because of the principle which I made reference to at the outset of this judgement (that the prosecutor does not advocate a particular sentence) to the probation officer then providing that assistance.

Of course, the probation officer shall not indicate that a particular fine should be imposed, nor is it his responsibility to decide whether or not the order which has been made should be or may be revoked, or in a case where the Crown Court is involved whether the offender should be committed to the Crown Court. However, what he can properly do in my view, based on his experience of supervising the offender who was the subject of the community service order, is assist the court as to whether or not there is any purpose in his view, as an experienced probation officer, in the community service order being allowed to continue. Sometimes he may take the view that a purpose could be served and he will then give the benefit of that view to the court; in other cases he may not'.

Nevertheless, it may be routine local practice for a different worker to assume the role of assessing the offender afresh and advising the court, particularly in regard to breach of a probation or supervision order.

Breach Reports

It is customary for the responsible officer to prepare a written 'breach report' which serves both to convey information conveniently to the court, minimising reliance on oral presentation, and to brief the court duty officer who may represent the responsible officer at court. It can also serve to inform the defence of the nature of the prosecution case and the wider view of the offender and their suitability or otherwise for the order's continuance. It is important to draft these with some care, remembering that there are two distinct elements or phases of the prosecution:

(a)   establishing or outlining the failure to comply, and

(b)   assisting the court in deciding how to exercise its powers.

There is often some tendency for responsible officers to conflate the two issues. First, remember that the breach report is not to be read by the court in helping it to decide whether a breach or failure to comply has occurred; it will be read only after the breach has been established.

Second, it is helpful to structure the report as follows:

(a)   Summarise the nature and origin of the order, licence or notice of supervision, its duration (and any expiry date) and the period during which the author has held statutory responsibility.

(b)   Outline the failure to comply, including pertinent details (including date(s) where appropriate) of the instruction(s) given and whether this followed formal warnings for earlier default, or earlier breach proceedings. It is not appropriate or relevant in this context to weave in references to other instances of alleged failures to comply which have not been the subject of enforcement proceedings and which the offender does not have a full opportunity to challenge or contest. Such references can simply be prejudicial without informing the court's view of the breach complaint before it.

(c)   Indicate, if appropriate, the extent of completion of or compliance with the order at the point where breach proceedings were initiated.

(d)   Explain the extent of the offender's compliance with the order since the prosecution was commenced, including (in the case of CS) the total number of hours so far worked and still outstanding.

(e)   Give a view of whether the order has a continuing, viable future or not, with reasons. If yes, it may be helpful to consider whether the offender would be suitable for (further or fresh) hours of community service (or attendance centre, if appropriate) as a penalty for the breach. You may also wish to indicate how the order would be proceeded with to maximise its prospects of successful completion.

(f)   It may be necessary to indicate in what way the order, if to continue, may need to be amended, *eg* by substitution of a fresh PSA, by extension of time limits (CS only) or by deletion or substitution of a requirement.

The breach report may well be overtaken by events and become outdated, *eg* if the grounds of the allegation are amended, or if the offender has since re-engaged with the requirements of the order, or if the offender's circumstances have altered significantly. This may mean that it will not be helpful to submit it and the responsible officer or the court duty officer should instead make an oral presentation. This may be particularly appropriate if an initial view that the order will probably need to be revoked has been superseded by a more considered judgement that the order has continuing worth.

Penalties for Breach

If the breach of a community order is admitted or proved but the court determines that the order should continue, the court may impose a separate penalty for each instance of breach which has been the subject of an information. Thus if four informations have been laid alleging failure to attend for community service work on four separate dates, the court could impose a fine or additional hours of community service for each date of absence. Similarly, if the offender is subject to two probation orders imposed on separate sentencing occasions and informations have been laid alleging a failure to attend for interview with the supervising officer on two occasions, making four informations in total (see page 5), four sets of penalties may be imposed.

In respect of a penalty of community service hours, the court's power is subject to a maximum aggregate of 60 hours or, where the relevant order is a CSO or a combination order, to the maximum permissible aggregate of hours combining both the orginal order and the additional penalty (see Chapters 3 and 4), whichever is the lower. If the breach is in respect of a YOI notice of supervision, where the court has power to impose a custodial sentence for a period not exceeding 30 days, the court may make custodial sentences in respect of more than one offence run concurrently or consecutively to each other up to a maximum of six months (MCA 1980 s133(1)), though it is highly unlikely that a court would deal with a breach by such a long term. A court may decide to impose a penalty for one or some of the breaches admitted or proved, opting to impose 'no separate penalty' in respect of the other matters.

Power of Revocation

If the court opts to revoke a community order in breach proceedings, it will require details of the offence(s) for which the order was imposed. These will be presented by the original prosecution agency, either the CPS or another agency such as the Department of Social Security or Customs and Excise. These agencies will not be prepared with the relevant papers unless they have been notified in advance by the enforcement agency that a breach prosecution is being pursued. Failure to notify is thus likely to cause delay, though the court may seek a fresh pre-sentence report in the meantime. Such delay will be inevitable if the offender appears unexpectedly on arrest on a warrant without bail but in respect of a summons or a warrant backed for bail, it is good practice to notify the CPS (or the alternative agency) of the details and date of the forthcoming hearing so that the file can be obtained in readiness. Where the CPS prosecuted the offence originally, notification is usually via the relevant department of the Police reponsible for administration of justice matters.

Remittal to Crown Court

Where a community order (other than a supervision order) was imposed by the Crown Court and the supervising court in breach proceedings does not consider it appropriate to deal with the failure to comply in a way which allows the order to continue, the court cannot revoke the order but may instead remit the matter (commonly referred to as committing the offender) back to the Crown Court, committing the offender to custody or releasing him or her on bail in the meantime. The probation prosecutor should send full details to the Crown Court liaison officer who will advise and make arrangements for representation by counsel at the Crown Court where necessary. When the offender appears before the Crown Court, and it is proved to the satisfaction of the court that s/he has failed to comply with any of the requirements of the order, the Crown Court has discretion to determine the appropriate course of action. A certificate signed by a justice of the peace certifying that the offender has failed to comply with the requirements of the relevant order shall be sent to the Crown Court, along with such other particulars of the case as may be desirable, and shall be admissible at Crown Court as evidence of the offender's failure to comply. Any question of whether the offender has failed to comply is a matter for the court and not for decision by a jury.

However, it is for the supervising court, not the Crown Court, to deal with any denial of breach or any claim by the defence of reasonable excuse. The Crown Court's need to be satisfied of the breach is a formal requirement rather than a basis for re-opening the substantive issue. If the offender claims at the Crown Court that their admission of breach before the supervising court was equivocal or otherwise open to doubt, the Crown Court is entitled to remit the case back to the supervising court and to order that court to rehear the case. The magistrates are not entitled to reject a direction of this nature. It is also open to the Crown Court to remit the matter back to the magistrates if the offender disagrees with the prosecution version of the facts of the breach but this will normally be resolved prior to the decision to remit the case or commit the offender. If the issue in disagreement only arises when the offender is before the Crown Court, the Crown Court may determine the matter for itself.

Bail Act Offence

If an offender fails to answer to bail, arising either from a warrant backed for bail or a remand by the court, this may constitute an offence under BA 1976 s6, punishable by fine or imprisonment (max. three months) or both. This is a unique offence and the relevant procedure was clarified by *Practice Direction (Bail: Failure to Surrender)* [1987] 1 WLR 79, the relvant paragraph (2) stating:

> Where a person has been granted bail by a court and subsequently fails to surrender to custody as contemplated by section 6(1) or (2) of the Bail Act 1976, on arrest that person should be brought before the court at which the proceedings in respect of which bail was granted are to be heard. It is neither necessary nor desirable to lay an information in order to commence proceedings for the failure to surrender. Having regard to the nature of the offence which is tantamount to the defiance of a court order, it is more appropriate that the court itself should initiate the proceedings by its own motion, following an express invitation by the prosecutor. The court will only be invited so to move if, having considered all the circumstances, the prosecutor considers proceedings are appropriate. Where a court complies with such an invitation, the prosecutor will naturally conduct the proceedings and, where the matter is contested, call the evidence. Any trial should normally take place immediately following the disposal of the proceedings in respect of which bail was granted.

As *Blackstone's Criminal Practice* (1994, p. 1050) points out:

> 'The indication in the *Practice Direction* that there should be a two-stage consideration of whether proceedings should be initiated (*ie*, the prosecutor decides whether to invite the court to proceed and the court then decides whether to act on his invitation) may not always coincide with practice. Many magistrates' courts informally ask the absconder or his legal representatve what the reason for his non-appearance was. If the explanation seems prima facie satisfactory, the bench indicates that no further action is necessary; otherwise the clerk is instructed to put the charge. The prosecution's views are not necessarily canvassed. Where a bench, on the occasion of an absconder's first appearance after his absconding, indicates, albeit informally, that no charge need be referred, that decision is binding on subsequent benches (*France v Dewsbury Magistrates' Court* [1988] Crim LR 295)'.

Taking the Oath

In enforcement proceedings a prosecutor needs to be sworn in four instances:

(a)　in laying a written information where a warrant is sought in the first instance;

(b)　in substantiating a written information not initially laid on oath where the offender has failed to attend court, either in answer to summons or after a simple adjournment in proceedings initiated by summons, and a warrant is now sought for the offender's arrest;

(c)　in giving evidence in contested proceedings;

(d)　in making any application or reference in respect of a supervision order where a summons cannot be served.

The form and manner of oath taking is regulated by the Oaths Act 1978, supplemented by established practice. The 'standard' form of oath is for the witness to take the New

Testament (or the Old Testament if the witness is a Jew) in their uplifted hand and to state:

> 'I swear by Almighty God that the evidence I shall give shall be the truth, the whole truth and nothing but the truth'.

Before a youth court the wording is slightly amended; instead of 'I swear by Almighty God...', the witness states 'I promise before Almighty God...'.

If the witness so chooses, the Scottish form of oath may be used, with the hand uplifted (without a Testament), stating:

> 'I swear by Almighty God, as I shall answer to God at the Great Day of Judgement, that I will speak the truth, the whole truth and nothing but the truth'.

If a witness objects to taking the oath in the standard form, the responsibility rests with them to indicate their preference but anyone who objects to being sworn is permitted to make 'solemn affirmation' instead (Oaths Act 1978 s5(1)) or to take the oath upon an alternate sacred text such as the Koran, the Vedas (for a Hindu) or the Granth (for a Sikh). If it is not reasonably practicable for a witness to be sworn in the manner appropriate to their religious belief, they should affirm instead (s 5(2)). If a person opts to affirm, they are not required to state the grounds of their objection. The words of affirmation are:

> 'I do solemnly, sincerely and truly declare and affirm that the evidence I shall give shall be the truth, the whole truth and nothing but the truth'.

As a professional in the courtroom, you will be expected to take the oath or affirm without prompting by the usher or clerk and it is helpful to commit the appropriate wording to memory.

Applications to Amend or Revoke/Discharge a Community Order and to Breach a Supervision Order

An information is neither necessary nor appropriate where the proceedings concern an application to amend or revoke/discharge a community order since proceedings of this nature are not concerned with any failure on the offender's part. Instead, in instances where the application is initiated by the responsible officer and the attendance of the offender is required, that officer should request the issue of a summons. In the case of alleged breach of a supersvion order, CYPA 1969 specifies that the supervisor shall proceed by application rather than by information. Here, too, the supervisor may request issue of summons. Only in the case of supervision order applications is the court empowered to issue a warrant in the first instance if satisfied that a summons cannot be served, though it is also possible in the enforcement of supervision orders for the supervisor to 'bring the supervised person before the court' (see page 60).

Practice Procedure

A typical procedural route to be followed by the responsible officer in instances where the offender's attendance at court is required is as follows:

(i)   Contact the 'listings' section at the justices' clerk's office to arrange a suitable date for a hearing, to be entered on the prospective summons.

(ii) Send four copies of the prospective summons to the justices' clerk. It is helpful though not essential to attach a photocopy of the relevant order.

(iii) After the summonses have been signed, three copies will be returned to the responsible officer.

(iv) One copy of the summons should be served on the offender, by one of the means outlined on page 8.

If the offender does not appear in answer to summons, a warrant for their arrest, backed or not backed for bail, may be issued. A format of summons for use in breach of supervision order proceedings is included in Chapter 5.

In instances where the offender's attendance at court is not required, *eg* applications to substitute a new PSA, the responsible officer should draft the amending order on the appropriate form and either write to the clerk to the justices enclosing three copies of the draft and requesting early consideration, or apply orally to the supervising court at a convenient opportunity, submitting the draft (three copies) for signature. This is detailed more fully in the relevant Chapters.

In revocation proceedings in respect of a Crown Court order, where the supervising court considers that the matter should be referred back to the Crown Court, the probation prosecutor should send full details to the Crown Court liaison officer who will advise and make arrangements for representation by counsel at the Crown Court where necessary.

Where the enforcement agency applies for revocation or is aware that the offender is making such an application (except in respect of early termination of a probation order for good progress), and the court opts to revoke the order or to remit the offender, the court will require details of the offence(s) for which the order was imposed. The enforcement agency should therefore notify the relevant agency responsible for prosecution of that offence in advance so that a file can be available in readiness (see page 21). In respect of community orders regulated in common by CJA 1991 sch 2, application for revocation and, more rarely, amendment may be made 'on the spot' where the offender is before the court and application is considered appropriate in the light of sentence imposed on the offender by the court in respect of a further offence. See, for example, Chapter 2 page 38.

Enforcement and Parental Bind Over

Under CJA 1991 s58, the parent or guardian of a child or young person convicted of an offence may be ordered to enter into a recognizance of up to £1,000 to take proper care of the minor and exercise proper control of him/her. When the juvenile is aged under 16 the court is under a *duty* to impose such a bind over, if satisfied in the circumstances of the case that it would be desirable in the interests of preventing further offending by the juvenile. Little use has been made of this power and the procedure for enforcement is far from clear-cut. However, CJ POA 1994 extends the power, in cases where the juvenile is made subject to a community sentence, by enabling the court to include in the recognizance a provision that the parent or guardian ensures that the juvenile complies with the requirements of that sentence. A parent or guardian cannot be bound over unless they give their consent but if they refuse consent and the court considers that their refusal is unreasonable, they can be fined up to £1,000.

2.
PROBATION ORDERS

Designated as a community order by CJA 1991 s6(4)(a), the probation order remains governed by PCCA 1973 but regulated for enforcement purposes by the generic provisions of CJA 1991 sch 2.

Requirements of the Order

The particular requirements of an order are stated in a schedule to the order issued by the court. The standard requirement of a probation order, specified by PCCA 1973 s2(6), is that the offender:

> 'shall keep in touch with the probation officer responsible for his or her supervision in accordance with such instructions as s/he may from time to time be given by that officer and should notify him or her of any change of address'.

Instructions will in the first instance be with regard to the keeping of appointments. It is noteworthy that the requirement to 'receive visits from the probation officer at home' pertaining prior to the 1991 Act is no longer specified and it is open to question whether the supervising officer can instruct the offender to receive such a visit. The *National Standard* of 1992 made no mention of home visits as a feature of supervision though whether this was because of the questionable enforceability of such an intervention is not apparent. Clearly a home visit will only be a helpful experience if the offender is agreeable and thus will normally proceed by negotiation and consent, but it is important to consider whether a probation officer can assert any statutory authority to seek such an encounter. The 1994 revised version of the *National Standard* asserts that a home visit is a 'method' of supervision and specifies that 'at least one home visit should take place in all cases' (para. 15), subject to health and safety considerations ('If risk to the officer is identified, it may be necessary to make special arrangements'). Instructions can also cover not just the 'when and where' but also the 'how', *ie* the standard of behaviour and language which is expected in the course of supervision or when otherwise on probation service premises or when accompanied by probation personnel, to prohibit language or behaviour that might reasonably give rise to serious offence to probation staff, other service users or members of the public. An instruction may also be necessary that the offender should not be under the influence of alcohol or non-prescribed drugs when attending appointments.

Additional Requirements

Additional requirements will almost always be cast within the specific provisions of PCCA 1973 sch 1A:

Residence (para. 1) This requirement will usually refer to residence at an approved probation hostel or another form of residential rehabilitation ('any other institution'), for a period specified in the order. Para. 1(1) is silent as regards a resident's compliance with rules and simply refers to inclusion of 'requirements as to the residence of the offender'. A requirement to abide by or comply with the rules of the hostel or institution is properly within the ambit of the sub-paragraph. However, this does not give the hostel or institution complete discretion in the casting of rules, as these must be reasonably related to the viability of residence and should not seek to impose controls outside of that legitimate territory. Thus a rule prohibiting either the consumption or the bringing of alcohol into the hostel or returning to the hostel intoxicated is a valid and relevant rule affecting residence, but a rule prohibiting residents from drinking in public houses would exceed the scope of the sub-paragraph. It is also proper to prohibit theft or damage to property within the hostel, or violent, threatening or oppressive behaviour or language whether towards staff or other residents outside of the hostel, as these affect the life of the establishment. Whether a rule could legitimately prohibit racist or sexist abuse towards a member of the public outside of the hostel is open to doubt, unless this misbehaviour occurs during the course of organised hostel activity. For a resident under age 18, a rule may require their participation in a government scheme of employment training. As this will be designed to ensure that they qualify for state benefit and are thus able to pay their residence charges, this is a legitimate rule relating to residence.

Activities (para. 2) This paragraph covers a range of possible requirements:

(a)   to present him or herself to a specified person at a specified place for not more than 60 days;

(b)   to participate in specified activities for not more than 60 days;

(c)   to refrain from participating in specified activities for the probation period or such portion as is specified.

Requirements (a) and (b) are to be in accordance with instructions given by the supervising officer and also require the offender, while participating, to comply with instructions given by or under the authority of the person in charge of the place or activities.

Probation Centre (para. 3) This operates to require attendance in accordance with instructions given by the supervising officer for not more than 60 days and, while attending, to comply with instructions given by or under the authority of the person in charge of the centre.

Treatment for Mental Condition (para. 5) This requirement is to 'submit to treatment by or under the direction of a qualified medical practitioner with a view to the improvement of the offender's mental condition' (para. 5(2)).

Treatment for Drug or Alcohol Dependency (para. 6) Couched in very similar terms to para. 5 requirements, this requirement is to 'submit to treatment by or under the direction of a person having the necessary qualifications or experience with a view to the reduction or elimination of the offender's dependency on drugs or alcohol' (para. 6(2)).

General Power Courts have a residual power under PCCA 1973 s3(1) to require the offender to comply with 'such requirements as the court... considers desirable in the interests of securing the rehabilitation of the offender or protecting the public from harm from the offender or preventing the commission by him or her of further offences', during the whole or any part of the probation period. Use of this provision will be extremely limited and the insertion of any requirement that cannot be devised within the ambit of sch 1A is probably inadvisable. In all instances requirements should be:

(a)   capable of precise and reasonable instruction;

(b)   open to ready oversight and enforcement;

(c)   confined within well-defined limits and should not confer undue discretion upon the supervising officer.

Jurisdiction

The order specifies the petty sessions area in which the offender resides or will reside (PCCA 1973 s2(2)). Jurisdiction to deal with enforcement proceedings lies with a magistrates' court (the supervising court), either a youth court or an adult magistrates' court depending on the age of the offender at the time when proceedings are initiated, acting for the specified PSA. The supervising court has the jurisdiction to deal with all aspects of enforcement proceedings save revocation of a Crown Court order either in breach or revocation proceedings. In all instances only the Crown Court may revoke an order imposed by that Court. The only power exercisable by another magistrates' court is the limited scope under sch 2 para. 9 to act when sentencing the offender to a custodial term for a further offence, either to revoke a magistrates' court order or, in the case of a Crown Court order, to remit the offender to the Crown Court.

Amending the Order

No application may be made while an appeal against the order is pending (sch 2 para. 16).

Substituting another PSA

Where the supervising court is satisfied that the offender proposes to change or has changed residence to another petty sessions area, the court may, and on the application of the supervising officer shall, amend the order by substituting the other PSA for the area specified (sch 2 para. 12(1) and (2)). The effect is that judicial oversight and jurisdiction for enforcement purposes will be exercised by a court acting for the new PSA.

This usually straightforward procedure is qualified by para. 12(3):

> The court shall not amend under this paragraph a probation order which contains requirements which, in the opinion of the court, cannot be complied with unless the offender continues to reside in the PSA concerned unless, in accordance with para. 13, it either:
>
> (a)   cancels those requirements; or
>
> (b)   substitutes for those requirements other requirements which can be complied with if the offender ceases to reside in that area.

In making application, the supervising officer should thus check the schedule of the order beforehand and be ready to answer the court if asked whether there are any additional requirements which will be affected by the transfer. If there are such conditions, the transfer application may need to be preceded by another application to amend a requirement of the order, as the following examples illustrate.

Illustration 1 If the order contains a requirement that the offender shall participate in an alcohol education programme for not more than 60 days or shall reside at a hostel for six months and moves address after completion of the requirement, a substitution of PSA will be straightforward without need of any prior amendment of requirements.

Illustration 2 If the order contains a requirement that the offender shall attend at a named probation centre for not more than 60 days and, prior to completion of that centre programme, the offender moves to another area the substitution of PSA amendment should not proceed unless the court also amends the order by, for example, deleting the existing requirement of probation centre attendance and inserting a requirement to attend a probation centre functioning in the new area.

Illustration 3 If the order in respect of an offender convicted of a sexual offence contains a requirement that the offender shall participate in a sex offender treatment programme for a year and after three months the offender moves to a new area where a programme of this nature is not available, the substitution of PSA amendment should not proceed unless the court also amends the order by deleting the requirement of programme participation. If deletion of the requirement would amount to a negation of the fundamental rationale of the order, the supervising court may feel that a deletion amendment is not appropriate and that it is preferable for the order to be revoked and the offender re-sentenced. Of course, the supervising court does not have power of revocation upon its own initiative, only upon application by the supervising officer or the offender. If the offender is not moving a substantial distance away, it may be possible for them to continue participation in the programme, in which case either the requirement can continue despite the substitution of PSA or this will constitute 'special circumstances' under which the offender should remain subject to the supervision of the current probation officer and the jurisdiction of the existing supervising court (PR 1984 r39(3)(b), see below).

Procedure In instances of simple amendment by substitution of PSA, the procedure is normally entirely straightforward. The offender is not required to be summonsed or to attend when the application is considered or to consent to the amendments (sch 2 para. 17(2)). The supervising officer can either:

(a) Write to the clerk to the justices giving details of the *offender* (name, age and new address), the *order* (date made, at which court, for what duration, the currently specified PSA) and the proposed amendment. This can be effectively conveyed by filling out a draft order of amendment (three copies) as specified by MA(CJA 1991)(MA)R 1992 Form 920. The proposed amendment on the form will, for example, state: 'By substituting the Borchester petty sessions area'. With the draft order send a covering letter outlining the change of circumstances which make the application appropriate; or

(b) If convenient, make an oral application (through the court duty officer if this is preferable) before an appropriate court, submitting the draft order as above (three copies) and outlining the basis of the application in oral presentation.

The court will almost certainly be 'satisfied' that the amendment is appropriate by the very nature of the supervising officer's application, without requiring any greater evidence of the change of residence. Once the order is amended, the clerk should give two copies of the amending order to the applicant and the supervising officer should give a copy to the offender and supply the other to the new supervising officer or the senior probation officer for the new area of residence. The clerk will send a copy of the amending order to the clerk to the justices for the new petty sessions area.

Para. 12 does not specify that an application may be made by the offender. This would nevertheless seem an implicitly valid if unlikely initiative.

Though the supervising officer has a duty under PR 1984 r39(1) and (2) to apply for an amendment of this nature, this is qualified by r39(3) which specifies that an application should not be made if:

(a)   the probation officer has reason to believe that the offender is unlikely to reside in the new area for a reasonable time; or

(b)   the probation officer has ascertained from the supervising court and the court acting for the PSA where the offender will reside that both courts are satisfied that, 'having regard to the special circumstances of the case, it is desirable that the person should remain under his or her supervision'.

Complications arise if the offender is moving to Scotland or Northern Ireland, thus requiring the special provisions of CJA 1991 sch 3 paras. 1 or 2.

Scotland The supervising court will need to be satisfied that suitable arrangements for the offender's supervision can be made by the regional or islands council for the offender's new area. The order on amendment shall specify the 'locality' of the new residence and, as the appropriate court for the purposes of Scottish legislation, a court of summary jurisdiction having jurisdiction in the specified locality. In the case of an offender convicted on indictment, the appropriate court will always be the sheriff court for that locality. In other instances, consult the Social Work Department in the offender's new locality. Though the provisions of PCCA 1973 sch 1A are generally transferable, subject to minor change of terminology (for 'probation officer' read 'an officer of the regional or islands council in whose area the offender will be residing') there is one difference of real substance – there is no provision in Scotland for attendance at a probation centre under sch 1A para. 3, so such a requirement in the order would need to be deleted. The 'home court' in Scotland thereafter having powers of enforcement will be the sheriff court (sch 3 para. 6(8)(a)).

Northern Ireland The supervising court will need to be satisfied that suitable arrangements for the offender's supervision can be made by the Probation Board for Northern Ireland. The order on amendment shall specify the appropriate petty sessions district in which the offender will be residing. Requirements inserted under PCCA 1973 sch 1A are generally transferable, subject to minor changes of terminology. References to a probation centre are to be treated as references to a 'day centre' as defined by Probation Act (NI) 1950 s2B. The 'home court' for enforcement purposes will be the court of summary jurisdiction acting for the specified petty sessions district.

In either instance, the advice of colleagues in the new area should be sought to ensure that the draft order of amendment is accurate. Note that though the 'home court' gains jurisdiction for purposes of enforcing the order after transfer, if that court is satisfied that the offender has failed to comply with any of the requirements of the order, it can require the offender to appear before the court in England or Wales which made the order, where this is considered to be in the interests of justice (sch 3 para. 6(5)). The court which made the order may then issue a warrant for the offender's arrest and may exercise any power which it could exercise in respect of the order if the offender resided in England and Wales (para. 6(6)).

If the offender moves to either the Channel Islands or the Isle of Man there is no provision for a transfer amendment. It may, however, be possible to negotiate with the Probation Service there to undertake supervision on behalf of the formal supervising officer, jurisdiction being retained by the current specified PSA. This may be a convenient device if the offender is simply working there temporarily but, if the move is permanent, a revocation application may be more appropriate.

Variation of Requirements

The supervising court is authorised by sch 2 para. 13(1) to exercise the following powers of variation:

    (a)   cancelling any of the requirements in the order; or

    (b)   inserting in the order (either in *addition* or in *substitution* for any such requirement) any requirement which the court could include if it were then making the order.

There are three variations which the court cannot make (para. 13(2)(a)):

    (a)   reducing the length of the probation period;

    (b)   extending the length of the probation period beyond three years from the date of the original order;

    (c)   inserting a requirement under PCCA 1973 sch 1A paras. 5 or 6 that the offender shall submit to treatment for mental condition or dependency on drugs or alcohol, *unless* the amending order is made within three months of the date of the original order.

If an offender has been subject to a requirement of probation hostel residence which has expired or is about to expire, is it possible to see the insertion of a further requirement of that nature or the extension of the time limit of the existing requirement? It has been drawn to the writer's attention that a court declined such an application, on the grounds that it has no power to make such an amendment, but it is difficult to see why such an amendment should not be made within the broad ambit of para.13(1)(b).

Power of variation is exercisable upon the application of either the supervising officer or the offender. PR 1984 r39(4) requires the supervising officer to make an application where such application for amendment can properly be made, unless the offender makes application first. In regard to a requirement of treatment either for mental condition or dependency on drugs or alcohol, the supervising officer is under a special duty to seek amendment in the circumstances specified by sch 2 para. 14:

(1) Where the medical practitioner or other person by whom or under whose direction an offender is being treated for his or her mental condition, or his or her dependency on drugs or alcohol, in pursuance of any requirement of a probation order:

    (a) is of the opinion mentioned in sub-paragraph (2) below; or

    (b) is for any reason unwilling to continue to treat or direct the treatment of the offender,

s/he shall make a report in writing to that effect to the responsible officer and that officer shall apply under paragraph 13 above to a magistrates' court for the petty sessions area concerned for the variation or cancellation of the requirement.

(2) The opinion referred to in sub-paragraph (1) above is:

    (a) that the treatment of the offender should be continued beyond the period specified in that behalf in the order;

    (b) that the offender needs different treatment, being treatment of a kind to which s/he could be required to submit in pursuance of a probation order;

    (c) that the offender is not susceptible to treatment; or

    (d) that the offender does not require further treatment.

Procedure Exercise of para. 13 powers of amendment requires the attendance of the offender, except in the following instances (para. 17(2)):

    (a)   cancelling a requirement of the order; or

    (b)   reducing the period of any requirement.

In all other instances, where the application is made by the supervising officer, the court:

    (a)   shall summon the offender to appear before the court; and

    (b)   if s/he does not appear in answer to the summons, may issue a warrant for his/her arrest.

The sought amendment may not be made unless the offender expresses willingness to comply with the requirements of the order as amended (para. 17(1)). If the application is made by the offender, the schedule makes no formal provision for the supervising officer to be notified or consulted but it is highly unlikely that the court would grant such an application without giving the supervising officer the opportunity to be heard.

Restriction on Liberty An amendment which adds a requirement will necessarily increase the restrictions upon the offender's liberty yet sch 2 does not require the court to consider the provisions of CJA 1991 s6(2)(b) regarding commensurability with the seriousness of the offence. If the original order was deemed to impose restrictions on liberty commensurate with the seriousness of the offence, it is questionable on what basis additional restrictions can be added. The only logical answer would seem to be that if the restrictions contained in the original order fell below the ceiling demanded by commensurability, in the light of considerations of suitability and the offender's personal circumstances, but those circumstances have now changed, then the offender could now be considered suitable for additional requirements, provided that these do not exceed that ceiling. As the offender must consent and thus has, in effect, a power of veto, such considerations are unlikely to arise frequently in practice. Consent is only likely to be forthcoming if the amendment is considered desirable to gain access to facilities or resources which would not be available unless linked to a formal statutory requirement.

Breach of the Order

Grounds for Prosecution

The particular statutory grounds on which a breach may be alleged are:

    (a)   failure to keep in touch with the supervising officer in accordance with instructions;

(b)   failure to notify the supervising officer of a change of address;

(c)   failure to comply with any additional requirement of the order.

'Instructions' A failure under (a) above is most likely to arise where the offender has failed to keep an appointment with the supervising officer (or with another officer designated by the supervising officer) or arrives unacceptably late for an appointment without notice or excuse. This will usually mean an office appointment but the basis of breach may be that the offender has not been at home to receive a visit from the supervising officer as reasonably notified and requested (see the discussion relating to home visits on page 25). The instruction may require the offender to maintain contact with a probation officer or member of staff other than the supervising officer, *eg* where the offender is temporarily away from their home area and it is appropriate that s/he should report to the most convenient office in the other area, or while the supervising officer is absent from work. The instruction should make clear that it is issued with the authority of the supervising officer and that further instructions given by the temporary supervisor carry the same authority as the supervising officer's instructions.

A prosecution is less straightforward where the allegation is grounded on unacceptable behaviour while the offender is fulfilling probation requirements. If the offender is subject to an additional requirement to attend a probation centre or to participate in activities/present him or herself to a specified person, PCCA 1973 sch 1A paras. 2 and 3 specifically require the offender 'to comply with instructions given by or under the authority of the person in charge'. Instructions can thus include a prohibition of language or conduct that might reasonably give serious offence to probation staff, other persons under supervision or members of the public (as per the *National Standard for Community Service Orders*, 1994 para. 14). Appropriate instruction may also be necessary where an offender persists in keeping appointments whilst inebriated or under the influence of drugs and thus unable to participate in meaningful discussion. In a prosecution based on failure to comply with an instruction to attend sober or not under the influence of non-prescribed drugs, the offender may, of course, claim 'reasonable excuse' that they suffered a dependency on alcohol or drugs and that their non-compliance was simply consistent with that condition. In this instance, recourse to revocation proceedings may be necessary instead of to breach action. In the case of a standard probation order, it is open to the supervising officer to build that form of expectation or prohibition into the instruction(s) given to the offender. Note that sch 1A paras. 5 and 6 (treatment for mental condition or for drug or alcohol dependency) do not specifically require compliance with instructions of the person responsible for the treatment, merely 'submission to treatment' and so the basis for breach on the ground of offensive language or behaviour whilst undergoing treatment is not apparent, albeit that this causes the person responsible to refuse to continue treatment (and thus necessitating an application for amendment under sch 2 para. 14). In all instances of breach based on grounds of offensive conduct or language, the prosecution may be open to challenge that the instruction was insufficiently clear and unambiguous to cover the misbehaviour in question or was not a reasonable instruction in the circumstances (see the discussion of this point in regard to community service orders, on page 47).

Reasonable Refusal to Comply An offender who is required to receive treatment for their mental condition or for dependency on drugs or alcohol under sch 1A para. 5 or 6:

shall not be treated... as having failed to comply with that requirement on the ground only that s/he has refused to undergo any surgical, electrical or other treatment if, in the opinion of the court, his or her refusal was reasonable having regard to all the circumstances (sch 2 para. 5(3)).

Though this is not explicit in regard to any other probation order requirement, the defence may seek to contest the allegation by suggesting that the instruction in question was unreasonable in the circumstances. This might apply, for example, to an instruction in the course of a group programme. In a well publicised case involving a requirement to attend a probation centre, the offender claimed in court that he had been expected to roleplay an orange in a group exercise and that this was an unreasonable demand. In a less exotic context, if a probation centre programme includes a practical work component, a probationer might seek to avoid such work activities on health grounds. Medical evidence of the offender's illness or disorder could provide a basis of 'reasonable excuse' for non-participation but would probably not provide a basis for avoidance of the whole of the programme's activities.

Non-Judicial Enforcement

The *National Standard* (1994, paras. 22–24) specifies as follows:

- any apparent failure to comply should be followed up within two working days;

- prosecution may be appropriate immediately in sufficiently serious instances of failure to comply, such as an attempt to avoid completion of the order or serious misconduct;

- if prosecution is not initiated on the first occasion of failure to comply, a formal warning should be given of the likely consequences of further failure to comply. The warning should be given in person, confirmed in writing and a copy placed on the offender's record. The supervising officer should confirm that the offender has clearly understood the warning and note the offender's response on the record;

- At most two warnings may be given before breach proceedings are instituted.

Initiating Prosecution

Prosecution is initiated in the normal manner by laying an information, seeking a summons or a warrant (see page 6), using Forms 92I, J and K (MC(CJA 1991)(MA) R 1992) as appropriate. A sample draft of an information using 92I is provided in Chapter 1. The alleged failure to comply with requirement(s) will, for example, state:

'Having been instructed on 3 September 1994 to attend for interview with the supervising officer on 12 September 1994, s/he failed to do so'.

'Failed to reside where directed by the supervising officer, leaving the Sunnyside Drug Rehabilitation Unit on 3 November 1994 without the knowledge or authorisation of the supervising officer'.

'Failed to comply with instructions given by the person in charge of the Michael Howard Probation Centre at Eastminster, smoking cannabis on the premises of the Centre on 5 October 1994, contrary to an instruction that no non-prescribed drugs should be used while attending the Centre'.

'Failed to notify the supervising officer of a change of address, leaving his/her last known address between 1 May and 15 May 1994 without informing the supervising officer'.

Note that, unlike the case of a community service order, there is no provision within the *National Standard* for the offender to be suspended from their requirement of compliance with instructions pending the outcome of the prosecution, though clearly this is a matter for the discretion of the supervising officer or the person in charge and may be necessary in the case of a requirement to attend a probation centre or an activity programme where gross misconduct is alleged.

Special considerations arise in the case of an offender with a requirement of hostel residence. Withdrawal of their hostel place will almost inevitably have substantial practical consequences for the offender yet the alleged breach has not yet been established in court and may be contested. Furthermore, the gross misconduct may be very difficult to substantiate, for example bullying, intimidation or violence toward another resident where the individual concerned is unwilling to give evidence about such victimisation. It may, nevertheless, be essential to remove or evict the offender quickly from residency. It may be possible to arrange their transfer to another hostel, making application for amendment of their order. Failing that, it is common practice for the resident to be evicted and for breach proceedings to be brought on the ground of their 'failure to reside', as they have rendered themselves ineligible for further residency.

Powers of the Supervising Court

If breach of the order is admitted or proved, the powers of the supervising court depend on:

(a)   whether the court opts to allow the order to continue (either in the existing or an amended form) or decides that the order should be revoked;

(b)   whether the order was made by a magistrates' court (youth or adult) or the Crown Court.

Where the Order will Continue If the court decides, in the light of the advice of the supervising officer concerning the offender's response to the order so far and the future viability of the order, and any representations by or on behalf of the offender that the order should be given a further chance, the offender may be dealt with 'in any one of the following ways' (sch 2 para. 3(1)):

(a)   a fine not exceeding £1,000;

(b)   a community service order for a number of hours 'not exceeding 60 in the aggregate' (para. 6(3)(a)).(As a CSO as a community order can be imposed only for an imprisonable offence, it seems to follow that a CSO would not be appropriate for breach of a probation order imposed for a non-imprisonable offence.);

(c)   if the offender is of an eligible age 'and the case is one to which CJA 1982 s17 applies', an attendance centre order for the period permissible under CJA 1982 s17 (12–36 hours). (As CJA 1982 s17 permits an attendance centre order to be imposed only for an imprisonable offence, it seems to follow that an ACO would not be appropriate for breach of a probation order imposed for a non-imprisonable offence.)

Uncertainty is sometimes expressed whether a court may opt instead to impose no penalty for the breach but instead simply reinforce the order with a warning about future conduct. Some clerks take the view that a penalty must be imposed, even if only a nominal fine. The wording of para. 3(1) that 'the court may deal with (the offender)' in either of the three ways outlined strongly suggests that the court is not obliged to exercise one of these powers. This interpretation was supported by the *National Standard* (1994 first draft, para. 80). The question will probably only arise where the failure to comply is of a very minor nature or arose out of unusual circumstances of a temporary nature, or where the offender has failed to comply in a number of instances and the court wishes to impose no separate penalty for one or more of those instances.

Use of Adjournment After a breach has been admitted or proved, the court may be uncertain whether the order has a viable future or not, particularly where the offender has not had recent contact with the supervising officer but now maintains that s/he is resolved to renew commitment to the order. The court may opt to adjourn proceedings for a convenient period to give the supervising officer the opportunity to reassess the situation with the offender and to test their commitment to co-operate. This procedure has the merit of keeping the prosecution alive before the court and the option, if the offender fails to comply, to proceed to revoke the order or (in the case of a Crown Court order) to remit the matter to the Crown Court (as outlined below). Some clerks or courts may discourage this form of delay, feeling that the matter should be resolved as quickly as possible, either by a penalty to mark the breach or by termination or by placing the issue before the Crown Court to adjudicate.

Power of Revocation If the order was imposed by a magistrates' court and the supervising court concludes that the order has ceased to be viable or should be terminated, the court:

may revoke the order and deal with (the offender), for the offence in respect of which the order was made, in any manner in which it could deal with the offender if s/he had just been convicted by the court of the offence (para. 3(1)(a)).

The court does not have the option to revoke without dealing with the offender afresh.

Crown Court Order: Power to Remit A magistrates' court has no power to revoke an order made by the Crown Court but may instead remit the offender back to the Crown Court, committing the offender to custody or releasing him/her on bail until s/he can be brought or appear before the Crown Court (para. 3(3)).

Powers of the Crown Court

Where an offender has been remitted to the Crown Court and:

it is proved to the satisfaction of the court that he has failed to comply with any of the requirements of the relevant order, that court may deal with him in respect of the failure in any one of the following ways (para. 4(1)):

(a)   impose a fine not exceeding £1,000;

(b)   make a community service order for a number of hours 'not exceeding 60 in the aggregate' (para. 6(3)(a));

(c)   if the offender is of an eligible age, make an attendance centre order for the period permissible under CJA 1982 s17 (12–36 hours);

(d)   'it may revoke the order and deal with the offender for the offence in respect of which the order was made, in any manner in which it could deal with the offender if s/he had just been convicted by or before the court of the offence' (para. 4(1)(d)).

The Crown Court has complete discretion and is not tied by the magistrates' decision not to allow the order to continue. It does not have the option simply to revoke without dealing with the offender afresh.

Community Service as a Penalty for Breach This is outlined in more detail in Chapter 3. It is probably more likely that such a penalty power will be used in respect of breach of a CSO than a probation order, as the court will in that instance have an existing basis for determining that the offender is suitable for community service. If CS is being considered for breach of probation then the court should hear from either a probation officer or a social worker to be 'satisfied that the offender is a suitable person to perform work under such an order' (PCCA 1973 s14(2), though this consultation is statutorily required only if 'the court thinks it necessary').

Attendance Centre as a Penalty for Breach Enforcement of such an order is governed by CJA 1982 ss17–19, as outlined in Chapter 6.

Re-Sentencing following Revocation

Because re-sentencing powers can also be exercised following a successful application for revocation, this somewhat complex issue is detailed separately in Chapter 8. In deciding how to deal with the offender, the court:

(a)   shall take into account the extent to which the offender has complied with the requirements of the relevant order; and

(b)   may assume, in the case of an offender who has wilfully and persistently failed to comply with those requirements, that s/he has refused to give his consent to a community sentence which has been proposed by the court and requires that consent (paras. 3(2) and 4(2)).

The provision in (b) links to CJA 1991 s1(3), as outlined in respect to breach of a community service order (page 52) but equally applicable in regard to a probation order.

Applications for Revocation

An application to revoke a probation order will be appropriate in the following circumstances:

(a)   good progress;

(b)   conviction of a further offence;

(c)   changed circumstances;

(d)   other instances where the order is no longer appropriate.

In each instance, the essential criterion for the court to consider is whether revocation 'would be in the interests of justice'.

Good Progress

This is appropriate where an offender has responded satisfactorily to the requirements of the order and early termination is sought as a mark of good progress and a recognition that the rehabilitative purpose of the order has been served. This possibility is explicitly acknowledged by sch 2 paras. 7(3) and 8(3):

> The circumstances in which a probation order may be revoked... shall include the offender's making good progress or his/her responding satisfactorily to supervision.

Revocation for this purpose is explicitly the exercise of 'simple' revocation under paras. 7(2) and 8(2)(a) without the offender being dealt with in some other manner for the offence in respect of which the order was made.

The *National Standard* of 1992 indicated that an application for early termination should not normally be sought before half-way through the term of the order but 'should be considered by two-thirds of the term unless there are clear reasons for not doing so'. This has been omitted in the revised 1994 version (para. 20(a)) which states:

> 'Early termination shall be considered where the offender has made good progress in achieving the objectives set out for the order and where there is not considered to be a significant risk of re-offending and/or of serious harm to the public'.

Conviction of a Further Offence

Though committing a further offence during the course of the order does not constitute a failure to comply with requirements, conviction of a further offence may provide appropriate grounds for a revocation application. This consideration will clearly arise where a custodial sentence has been imposed for that offence. The main consideration will be the length of the custodial term and the portion of that sentence which will be spent in actual custody, the demands of any statutory early release licence or supervision which the offender will face on release and the offender's resettlement plans. The supervising officer will need to judge whether it is appropriate for the order to remain in temporary abeyance while the offender is not at liberty, to be resumed on release, or should be terminated. The offender may also have a view on the issue and may wish to be released from custody without the burden of resuming a continuing commitment of this nature. An application may be possible on the same occasion as the custodial sentence is imposed or may need to be made subsequently.

An application is likely to be of particular merit where the offender has shown little motivation to make constructive use of supervision under the probation order and the subsequent custodial sentence provides a good opportunity to bring the order to an end. It should not be assumed, however, that a custodial sentence spells the demise of the order. The question must be considered on the facts of each individual case whether the order's continuance will serve any valid purpose. See, in this context, the Court of Appeal cases in *R v Rowsell* (1988) 10 Cr App R(S) 411 and *R v Cawley* (1994) 15 Cr App R(S) 209, detailed on page 81.

An application should also be considered appropriate where the offender has been sentenced not to a custodial term but to a further community sentence and it is felt desirable to rationalise the offender's commitments by terminating the existing order. Thus if the offender is sentenced to a probation order or combination order for the further offence, revocation of an existing probation order will be sensible to avoid the complexities and duplicating nature of two sets of supervisory requirements.

Changed Circumstances/No Longer Appropriate

Though this consideration will apply less frequently in regard to probation orders than community service orders, instances will arise where the offender's present circumstances render the continuation of the order no longer viable or appropriate. New circumstances of ill-health, disability, employment commitments or family commitments can usually be accommodated within the flexibility of the probation order unless the changed situation is of an extreme nature, *eg* the offender being stricken with a terminal illness or a highly restrictive disability, where it may seem sensible to remove the bind of supervisory commitment which is now essentially redundant or superfluous. The same might be said if the offender secures long-term employment abroad or seeks to emigrate. A further basis for seeking revocation could be where the offender has demonstrated, without failing to comply with a requirement, that the order has little positive merit or interest and they would prefer not to continue with a somewhat hollow commitment. In this instance the application might be more appropriately made by the offender but if this initiative is not forthcoming the supervising officer may opt to proceed.

Application Procedure

Application can be made by either the supervising officer or the offender in two instances:

(a)   at any stage during the order to a magistrates' court acting for the specified PSA (the supervising court) (para. 7(1));

(b)   to a magistrates' court other than the supervising court if the offender is convicted of a further offence by that other court and a custodial sentence is imposed (para. 9(1)). Though para. 9 does not specify the point at which an application should be made, the clear implication is that this will be appropriate on the occasion when the custodial sentence is passed. Though there seems nothing explicit to prohibit a subsequent application, if that opportunity is missed, para. 9 is silent as to how the offender is to be brought before the court. After the event, it will be altogether more appropriate and straightforward to make application to the supervising court, which has power not only to revoke but also to deal with the offender afresh. A magistrates' court other than the supervising court does not have this power.

If the application is made 'on the spot', *eg* in immediate response to the imposition of a custodial sentence, the application will normally be presented orally and, if the applicant is the supervising officer, or the court duty officer acting on their behalf, there is clearly no need to summon the offender who is already before the court. If, as is likely, a pre-sentence report is prepared for the new sentencing occasion, the supervising officer may opt to address the question of revocation in the report. If, however, this is felt to be undesirable, pre-judging the outcome of the case, an accompanying letter to the clerk can indicate a wish to make application in the event of a certain sentence being passed, which the clerk can then draw to the court's attention in the event that such a sentence is imposed.

In other instances, where application is made to the supervising court and the applicant is the supervising officer, the provisions of para. 7(7) apply:

> Where a magistrates' court proposes to exercise its powers under this paragraph otherwise than on the application of the offender it shall summon him or her to appear before the court and, if s/he does not appear in answer to the summons, may issue a warrant for his or her arrest.

A summons is sought in the normal manner (*not* by laying an information) (see page 7) using Form 92M specified by MC(CJA 1991)(MA)R 1992. There is no power to seek a warrant (Form 92N) in the first instance and in circumstances where a warrant would appear necessary, the appropriate action would almost certainly be a prosecution for breach (*eg* for failure to notify change of address) rather than a revocation application. If the application is prompted by the offender's conviction of a further offence resulting in a custodial sentence, a *production order* will need to be obtained by arrangement with the CPS so that the offender can be brought to court from the prison establishment in which they are serving sentence.

Considering an Application based on Good Progress

If application is made to the supervising court by the supervising officer, an application on this ground is no different from any other basis of application and the summons procedure of para. 7(7) must be followed to bring the offender before the court. It should not be necessary for them to appear in the dock. The court will expect a written or oral report from the supervisor outlining the progress achieved under the order, the offender's response to supervision and their present circumstances and prospects. Some courts may be willing to proceed to consider the application even if the offender does not answer to summons but the legitimacy of this is open to doubt.

Where the order was imposed by a magistrates' court and may thus be revoked by the supervising court, there may be a procedural advantage if the offender makes the necessary application, quite apart from any personal merit attributable to taking this responsibility. The summons process is avoided and the court may be willing to consider the offender's written application without need of their personal appearance, if the application is supported by the supervising officer, reporting on progress as outlined above. If the court then considers that it should not proceed in the offender's absence, the application may be adjourned to allow them to attend. If the offender then declines to attend in person, the application will doubtless be dismissed.

If the probation order was imposed by the Crown Court, sch 2 makes no differentiation and requires application to be made to the supervising court in the first instance which must then remit the matter back to the Crown Court, bailing the offender in the interim and thus exposing the offender to potential Bail Act liabilities. At some Crown Court centres this laborious and cumbersome process has been cut short by the resident judges who have indicated a willingness to consider applications in chambers on direct application by the supervising officer, backed by a progress report as above, obviating the need to apply via the supervising court. This is certainly labour-saving and cost effective, if of questionable legality. The Crown Court liaison officer will advise which procedure the local judiciary prefer.

Considering an Application based on Changed Circumstances

If the application is made to the supervising court by the supervising officer, the court will expect an oral or written report outlining the progress of the order to date and the change of circumstances which appear to make termination appropriate. An offender who wishes to avoid exposure to re-sentencing may seek to persuade the court that their circumstances now permit the worthwhile continuance of the order. The court may then opt to adjourn proceedings for a suitable period to test whether this argument has validity. Adjournment may be a simple adjournment without need of remand on bail if the offender has answered to summons.

If the court concludes that revocation would be in the interests of justice (*ie* the order has no viable future and should be terminated), the powers of the court depend on whether the probation order was imposed by the Crown Court or a magistrates' court. The supervising court may only revoke a magistrates' court order but in these circumstances has a choice of whether simply to revoke the order or to revoke and deal with the offender afresh for the original offence (para. 7(2)(a)). The former option may be chosen where the duration of the order has been substantially completed or the offender's changed circumstances and/or the lapse of time since the original offence and their absence of convictions in the interim persuade the court that re-sentencing would not be in the interests of justice. This is a matter on which the defence will doubtless seek to address the court. In the majority of instances the court will opt to revoke and deal afresh. The question will then arise whether a fresh pre-sentence report is required prior to re-sentencing.

If the order was imposed by the Crown Court, the supervising court must remit the matter to be considered by the Crown Court (para. 7(2)(b)).

The question of revocation and re-sentence is addressed more fully in Chapter 8.

Revocation or Breach Proceedings?

In some instances there may be doubt in the supervising officer's mind whether application should be made in revocation proceedings or a prosecution initiated in breach proceedings. This dilemma is illustrated in the context of a community service order by *R v Jackson* (1984) 6 Cr App R(S) 202, outlined on page 55. The Court of Appeal's view favouring breach action would appear equally valid in regard to a probation order. There will, nevertheless, be instances where an order is progressing unsatisfactorily yet revocation may be the only option. For example, an offender subject to a probation order may be continually moving around the country to such an extent that no basis of regular reporting and supervision can be established. If the offender is instructed to contact the probation office in each area where s/he is temporarily staying and duly does so, it could be very difficult to substantiate a breach allegation (even if he or she omits to report as instructed, it could be difficult to establish a failure to comply). Nevertheless, the order lacks any meaningful basis upon which to continue supervision.

Substitution of a Conditional Discharge

Prior to CJA 1991 it was common practice to make application under PCCA 1973 s11 for the probation order to be discharged and for a conditional discharge to be substituted in respect of the original offence. This was a popular choice where the supervising officer felt that the order could serve no further useful purpose but it was considered to be premature in the life of the order to seek outright termination. It is far from clear whether this option has survived the implementation of the 1991 Act. Though s11 was not repealed by that Act, s11(1) grants power of substitution to a court 'having power to discharge a probation order', yet power to discharge under PCCA 1973 s5(1) and sch 1 para. 1 was repealed by the Act (sch 13). Unless it can be maintained that 'discharge' should now be read as an implicit reference to 'revocation', s11 appears to have been rendered obsolete.

Under para. 7(2) revocation powers, a court revoking an order may deal with the offender in some other manner. This would allow a conditional discharge to be imposed for a period determined by the court, taking effect on the date it is ordered. This does not achieve the same effect as a s11 substitution because a conditional discharge substituted under that power has a retrospective effect as if it had been ordered on the date of the making of the probation order and continues for the duration of the probation period.

Other significant differences also pertain under s11 procedure:

(a)   The offender's attendance at court is not required provided that the supervising officer:

'produces to the court a statement that (the probationer) understands the effect of an order under s11 and consents to the application being made' (s11(3)).

(b)   The court has power only to discharge the order outright, to substitute a conditional discharge or to decline the application. Under para. 7(2), the court has complete discretion in how it will deal with the matter afresh.

(c)   Substitution can be made by the supervising court even if the probation order was imposed by the Crown Court (unless the Crown Court had specifically reserved power of discharging the order to itself). Under para. 7(2) revocation of a Crown Court order can only be granted by the Crown Court.

Pending an authoritative determination of the issue, any application under s11 will probably depend on the interpretation given by the local court.

Procedure Given the repeal of PCCA 1973 sch 1 para. 1, the procedure to be adopted in a s11 application, where the supervising court is willing to receive such an application, is unclear and a matter of local discretion. In the writer's local court, probation officers are advised to seek a summons, following the same procedure as when seeking to amend a probation order, but it is difficult to see why this process should apply under s11. If an offender is agreeable to the application, it seems open to the supervising officer to write to the court outlining the details of the order and the nature of the application, asking for a suitable date to be fixed for the application to be heard. The basis of the application can then be presented orally or in a written report, backed by the offender's signed statement of consent. If the court feels unable to proceed in the offender's absence, the matter can be adjourned to give them an opportunity to attend. If the offender is unwilling to consent or to attend, the summons procedure to enforce their attendance would seem an unwarrantedly heavy handed device, quite apart from being open to doubt as a legal procedure. In such instances the alternatives appear to be either to allow the probation order to continue or to initiate revocation proceedings.

3.
COMMUNITY SERVICE ORDERS

A community service order may be imposed on offenders aged 16 or over in two instances:

(a)   as a community order (CJA 1991 s6(4)(b));

(b)   as a penalty for the breach of a community order governed by CJA 1991 sch 2.

Though the order remains governed by PCCA 1973, supplemented by the Community Service and Combination Order Rules 1992, enforcement is regulated by the generic provisions of CJA 1991 sch 2.

Requirements of the Order

The core requirements of the order, specified by PCCA 1973 s15(1), are:

(a)   to keep in touch with the relevant officer in accordance with such instructions as s/he may from time to time be given by that officer;

(b)   to notify the relevant officer of any change of address;

(c)   to perform for the number of hours specified in the order such work at such times as s/he may be instructed by the relevant officer.

The 'relevant officer', as defined by PCCA 1973 s14(4), is either a designated probation officer or 'a person appointed... by the probation committee' serving the petty sessions area specified in the order. The relevant officer is the 'responsible officer' for enforcement purposes under CJA 1991 sch 2. The basic requirement to work is augmented by CSCOR 1992 r4(1):

> While performing work under an order an offender shall be required to comply with any reasonable directions of the supervisor as to the manner in which the work is to be performed and with any rules reasonably imposed by the supervisor in the place of work having regard to the circumstances of that workplace, the interests of health or safety or the interests and well-being of other persons present.

Instructions given by the relevant officer should, so far as practicable, avoid any conflict with the offender's religious beliefs and any interference with times at which s/he normally works or attends a school or other educational establishment (PCCA 1993 s15(3)).

Twelve Months Duration

PCCA 1973 s15

> (2) Subject to CJA 1991 sch 2 para. 15, the work required to be performed under a community service order shall be performed during the period of 12 months beginning with the date of the order but, unless revoked, the order shall remain in force until the offender has worked under it for the number of hours specified in it.

CJA 1991 sch 2 para. 15 makes provision for an order to be amended by extending the period of the order and is detailed below (page 45).

Note that the order comes into force as soon as the court has pronounced sentence and the offender is immediately subject to it, irrespective of whether or when a copy of the order is served on the offender. In *Walsh v Barlow* [1985] 1 WLR 90 an offender tried to argue that the order imposed on him was not effective as no copy of the order had been given to him but the Divisional Court held that such delivery is 'not a pre-requisite of the coming into force of the order'.

Enforcement Pending Appeal

An offender subject to a CSO who is appealing against their conviction or sentence may seek to be excused the obligations and requirements of the order pending the outcome of their appeal. In a letter to Chief Probation Officers (26 November 1992), the Home Office advised:

> 'The CSO remains in force until overturned or varied on appeal and should therefore be enforced in the normal way. There is no legal power enabling probation officers to suspend the order pending appeal'.

This advice has been widely adopted and an offender who failed to work as instructed in such circumstances would need to have recourse to the claim that their outstanding appeal constituted 'reasonable excuse' for non-compliance. Though the Home Office is correct that there is no legal power of suspension, the relevant officer retains discretion when and if to give work instructions, albeit that to postpone normal commencement of the order would be contrary to the *National Standard*.

Jurisdiction

The order specifies the petty sessions area in which the offender resides (or will reside) (PCCA 1973 s14(4)). Jurisdiction to deal with enforcement proceedings lies with a magistrates' court (the supervising court), either a youth court or an adult court depending on the age of the offender at the time when proceedings are initiated, acting for the specified PSA (sch 2 para. 1(1)(a)). This court has the jurisdiction to deal with all aspects of enforcement proceedings save revocation of a Crown Court order either in breach or revocation proceedings. In all instances only the Crown Court may revoke an order imposed by that Court. The only power exercisable by another magistrates' court is the limited scope to act when sentencing the offender to a custodial term for a further offence, either to revoke a magistrates' court order or, in the case of a Crown Court order, to remit the offender to the Crown Court.

Amending the Order

No application may be made while an appeal against the order is pending (sch 2 para. 16).

Substituting another PSA

Where the supervising court is satisfied that the offender proposes to change or has changed residence to another petty sessions area the court may, and on the application of the relevant officer shall, amend the order by substituting the other petty sessions area (sch 2 para. 12). The effect is that judicial oversight and jurisdiction for enforcement purposes will be exercised by a court acting for the new PSA.

Para. 12(4) requires that a court shall not make an amendment 'unless it appears to the court that provision can be made for the offender to perform work under the order under the arrangements which exist for persons who reside in the other petty sessions area to perform work under such orders'. This is very unlikely to create any difficulty as the national availability of work is so comprehensive but liaison and negotiation with the community service staff in the new area will clarify the position in the case of any doubt. In the rare instance that work arrangements cannot be made in the new area, the appropriate application is for revocation rather than amendment; jurisdictional responsibility should not be passed to a new court.

Procedure This is normally an entirely straightforward procedure. The offender is not required to be summonsed or to attend when the application is considered or to consent (sch 2 para. 17(2)). The relevant officer can either:

(a) Write to the clerk to the justices giving details of the *offender* (name, age and new address), the *order* (date made, at which court, for what duration, the currently specified PSA) and the proposed *amendment*. This can be effectively conveyed by filling out a draft order of amendment (three copies) as specified by MC(CJA 1991)(MA)R 1992 Form 920. The proposed amendment wording will, for example, state: 'By substituting the Borchester petty sessions area'. With the draft order send a covering letter outlining the change of circumstances which make the application appropriate and the availability of work in the new area; or

(b) If convenient, make an oral application (through the court duty officer if this is preferable) before an appropriate court, submitting the draft order as above (three copies) and outlining the basis of the application in oral presentation.

The court will almost certainly be 'satisfied' that the amendment is appropriate by the very nature of the relevant officer's application, without requiring any greater evidence of the change of residence. Once the order is amended, the clerk should give two copies of the amending order to the applicant and the relevant officer should give a copy to the offender and supply the other to the relevant officer for the new area of residence. The clerk will send a copy of the amending order to the clerk to the justices for the new petty sessions area. Para. 12 does not explicitly anticipate that an application may be made by the offender but this seems to be an implicitly valid if unlikely initiative.

Complications arise if the offender is moving to Scotland or Northern Ireland, thus requiring the special provisions of CJA 1991 sch 3 paras. 3 or 4.

Scotland The order on amendment shall specify the 'locality' of the new residence and shall require the regional or islands council in whose area that locality is situated to assign an officer to exercise responsibility under the Community Service by Offenders (Scotland) Act 1978. The 'home court' which will exercise jurisdiction will be the sheriff court for the offender's new locality.

Northern Ireland The order on amendment shall specify the 'petty sessions district' for the offender's new area and require the Probation Board for Northern Ireland to assign an officer to exercise responsibility under the Treatment of Offenders (NI) Order 1976. The 'home court' will be the court of summary jurisdiction acting for the petty sessions district. Because the maximum length of hours for an offender aged 16 remains 120 hours in

Northern Ireland, the court amending the order for a greater number of hours in respect of an offender aged 16 may amend the order by reducing the number of hours specified (sch 3 para. 4(2)).

There is no statutory provision for a CSO to be transferred to either the Isle of Man or the Channel Islands.

Extension of Order

CJA 1991 sch 2 para. 15

Where:

(a)   a community service order is in force in respect of any offender; and

(b)   on the application of the offender or the responsible officer, it appears to a magistrates' court acting for the petty sessions area concerned that it would be in the interests of justice to do so having regard to the circumstances which have arisen since the order was made,

the court may, in relation to the order, extend the period of 12 months specified in PCCA 1973 s15(2).

This power will be appropriately used where the offender's work performance has been interrupted by illness, employment demands, periods in custody etc, particularly for longer orders. An application may also be appropriate at the conclusion of breach proceedings where the order is to continue but the prosecution has been protracted and the offender has not worked in the interim. Note that s15(2) (cited on page 42) specifies that 'the order shall remain in force' until the offender has completed their hours. This means that work instructions can continue to be given and that breach and revocation proceedings can be initiated after 12 months have elapsed, even though no extension has been sought. This was confirmed by the Court of Appeal in *R v Tebbutt* (1988) 10 Cr App R(S) 88:

> 'The words... are designed to give a discretion to the community service organiser to allow the offender to continue with the work, although the 12 month period has elapsed. It is the organiser who is in control of the administration of the order and (the sub-section) leaves it to his discretion to decide whether to allow the offender to continue with the work...' (per Tudor Evans J, p92).

This might appear to make a para. 15 amendment superfluous. It is nevertheless good practice and sensible to seek a time extension because this avoids ambiguity and provides a helpful revised target date by which the obligation to complete the hours should be satisfied.

Para. 15 is open-ended and does not specify any maximum time span beyond which the order cannot be extended. It is not clear whether a second or further extension may be sought because para. 15 refers only to extending 'the period of 12 months'. This appears to limit the power to a one-off instance, so care should be taken to estimate the length of a proposed extension in a realistic way, allowing for possible interruptions.

The question whether an offender can be in breach for failure to complete their hours within 12 months (or the period by which the order is extended) is raised on page 47.

Procedure Though usually straightforward, this process requires the attendance of the offender and if the application is made by the relevant officer, the court shall issue a summons requiring the offender to appear (sch 2 para. 17(1)(a)). This should be sought and served by the usual procedure (see page 23). There is no alternative power to issue a warrant at the initiation of proceedings but a warrant may be issued if the offender does not answer to summons (para. 17(1)(b)). If the offender is already before the court (*eg* in breach proceedings) then an oral application can be made 'on the spot', by-passing the summons procedure. The amendment cannot be made unless the offender expresses 'willingness to comply' with the proposed extension (para. 17(1)). In this unlikely possibility, the application cannot proceed. The relevant officer should continue to instruct the offender to work and if, as seems likely, the offender defaults, breach proceedings can be initiated.

Breach of the Order

Grounds for Prosecution

The particular statutory grounds on which a breach may be alleged are:

(a)   failure to keep in touch with the relevant officer in accordance with instructions (this covers any failure to attend for interview either at the commencement of the order or to review progress at any stage);

(b)   failure to notify the relevant officer of any change of address;

(c)   failure to work at the times instructed by the relevant officer (this includes unauthorised late arrival for work and early departure or absence from the work site);

(d)   failure to comply with any reasonable work directions of the supervisor (this includes deliberate non-co-operation, sabotage or other obstructive behaviour which frustrates the purpose of the offender's or others' orders and work which, in the words of the *National Standard* (1994 para. 14), 'fails to demonstrate the required level of commitment');

(e)   failure to comply with a rule reasonably imposed by the supervisor in the interests of health or safety, or the interests and well-being of others present, whether supervisors, workers, beneficiaries or other members of the public.

Instructions issued by the relevant officer can include an instruction to work as directed by a community service unit elsewhere, *eg* where the offender is living for the time being away from their usual home area and it is possible for them to work within the scheme operating in that locality acting as agent for the relevant officer. The offender should be instructed by the relevant officer that instructions issued by the staff of the other unit carry the same authority as the relevant officer's instructions.

Directions by the supervisor can be issued by way of general rules setting out required standards of behaviour applicable throughout the period of community service and can encompass not just the prohibition of 'active' misbehaviour while engaged in CS work (*eg* a rule against fighting, consuming alcohol or taking non-prescribed drugs), but also the prohibition of 'passive' misbehaviour (*eg* a rule prohibiting attendance for work whilst under the influence of alcohol or non-prescribed drugs). It is therefore important that such rules are clearly explained to the offender and a copy supplied, so that it is possible subsequently to establish that a rule, instruction or direction was given and understood.

It is obvious that the more gross the misconduct, the more clearcut a breach allegation will be. The direction or rule has to be 'reasonable' and an offender or the defence may assert that the instruction was not 'reasonable' in the circumstances. It might also be claimed that the instruction was not sufficiently clear and unambiguous for the offender to know whether their behaviour was in fact misbehaviour. This difficulty is perhaps most likely to arise in respect of a rule prohibiting 'conduct or language that might reasonably give serious offence to probation staff, other persons under supervision or members of the public' (*National Standard*, 1994 para. 14). While the rule is designed to prevent sexist, racist or other oppressive language or harassment, it is worth considering how easy it would be in practice to assert the instruction in breach proceedings if the offender is alleged to have repeatedly made 'Irish jokes'. Clearly CS staff will seek to deal initially with such instances in a variety of constructive ways which will both emphasise and clarify the unacceptability of such language.

It is unclear whether it is a ground for breach that the offender failed to complete the specified hours within 12 months (or such period by which the order has been extended). This is not likely to be an issue in practice as non-completion will usually arise out of failure to work as instructed, giving sound grounds for breach action or because of the offender's continuing unavailability for work, thus constituting a basis for seeking revocation.

Reasonable Excuse : Sickness

The most common basis on which the offender may claim reasonable excuse for their failure to attend for work is that they were unfit to work at the relevant time because of illness or injury. Offenders will be routinely requested to obtain a medical certificate or a letter from their doctor promptly to support such claims. If no such proof is submitted and a prosecution ensues, it is still open to the offender to claim 'reasonable excuse' at court, usually backed by some form of written evidence. Whether such a claim in a disputed breach prosecution, not backed by medical evidence, will be accepted will be a matter for the court to decide. If, however, a doctor's note or certificate is produced, this is not necessarily decisive. The 'sick note' may be completed retrospectively to cover a previous period of claimed unfitness of which the doctor had no direct observation. Is the opinion based on a professional assessment of the offender's present condition which indicates the extent of their previous incapacity or is it formed entirely on the basis of the patient's own say-so? If the latter is suspected, the prosecution may wish to pursue the allegation so that the offender's failure to submit proof promptly can be considered by the court and any medical witness called on behalf of the offender can be questioned about the basis of their opinion.

In this context it might be argued that the offender's failure to supply a medical certificate promptly, if instructed to do so, was in itself a failure to comply with a requirement of the order and could thus provide the basis for a prosecution in its own right, whether or not the medical opinion provides solid support for a claim of reasonable excuse. Quite apart from this appearing a somewhat 'last resort' tactic, it is doubtful whether this is a prosecutable failure. The instruction is not a reasonable direction as to the manner in which work is performed or a rule imposed in the interests of health, safety or well-being. It is difficult to see that it constitutes an actionable demand upon the offender.

47

Non-Judicial Enforcement

The *National Standard* (1994, paras. 24–28) specifies as follows:

• any apparent failure to comply should be dealt with within two working days;

• prosecution should be initiated at any stage of the order (regardless of the number of hours still to be worked) and without prior warning, if the failure to comply is serious, involving either an attempt to avoid its completion or serious misconduct;

• if prosecution is not initiated on the first occasion of failure to comply, a formal warning should be given of the consequences of further failure, in person and confirmed in writing, a copy to be held on record together with a note of the offender's response;

• at most, two warnings may be given before breach proceedings are instituted.

Exclusion from Placement CSCOR 1992 r4(2) specifies:

Where an offender:

(a)   fails to comply with any such direction or rule as is mentioned in the preceding paragraph;

(b)   in any way fails satisfactorily to perform the work he has been instructed to do;

(c)   behaves in a disorderly or disruptive manner or in a manner likely to give offence to members of the public or any person for whose benefit the work is being performed; or

(d)   reports for work later than the appointed time

he may (without prejudice to any proceedings for failure to comply with the requirements of the order under schedule 2 to the Criminal Justice Act 1991) be required to cease work that day and may, in addition be required to leave the place of work forthwith; and where he is so required to cease work, the relevant officer may direct that some or all of any period of work for that day shall not be reckoned as time worked under the order.

The *National Standard* (1994, para. 26) adds:

'In the case of failure to comply, the supervisor may in addition require the offender to leave the placement and delete from the record any completed CS hours for that day'.

Sickness Absence Absence from work where sickness is claimed should be treated as failure to comply unless the relevant officer has reasonable grounds to believe that the sickness is genuine and serious enough to prevent attendance and that the offender has made reasonable efforts to contact the Probation Service to explain the circumstances (*National Standard*, 1994, para. 28).

Initiating Prosecution

If it is decided to take breach action, proceedings should be instituted within ten working days (*National Standard* 1994, para. 30). Prosecution is initiated in the normal manner by laying an information, seeking a summons or a warrant, using Forms 921, J and K (MC(CJA 1991)(MA)R 1992) as appropriate. A sample draft of an information is provided in Chapter One.

Suspension from Work Whether the offender should continue work when breach proceedings are in train is a matter of discretion. The *National Standard* (1994, para. 29) specifies:

'Offenders may be allowed to continue working…, provided this does not involve undue risk to the public, probation staff or other offenders and that they confirm that they will accept all the requirements of the order. It should be explained to the offender that it will be for the court to decide whether or not to revoke the order and to what extent the offender's conduct in the meantime should be taken into account when considering the breach'.

Suspension can further erode the offender's motivation to tackle the order and it is a serious step to remove the opportunity from the offender to demonstrate a renewed commitment or to earn potential mitigation in the event of revocation.

Powers of the Supervising Court

If breach of the order is admitted or proved, the powers of the supervising court depend on:

(a)   whether the court opts to allow the order to continue or decides that the order should be revoked;

(b)   whether the order was made by a magistrates' court (youth or adult) or the Crown Court.

Where the Order will Continue If the court decides, in the light of the advice of the relevant officer concerning the offender's response to the order so far, the extent of completion to date and the future viability of the order, and any representations from or on behalf of the offender that the order should be allowed to continue, the offender may be dealt with 'in any one of the following ways' (sch 2 para. 3(1)):

(a)   a fine not exceeding £1,000;

(b)   a community service order, for a number of hours 'not exceeding 60 in the aggregate' (para. 6(3)(a)).

Uncertainty is sometimes expressed whether a court may opt to impose no penalty for the breach but instead simply reinforce the order with a warning about future conduct. Some clerks take the view that a penalty must be imposed, even if only a low or nominal fine. The wording of para. 3(1) that 'the court *may* deal with (the offender)' in either of the two ways outlined strongly suggests that the court is not obliged to do one or other. This interpretation was supported by the *National Standard* (1994, first draft, para. 30). The question will probably arise only where the failure to comply is of a very minor nature or where the offender has completed the order satisfactorily since the prosecution was initiated, or where the offender has failed to comply in a number of instances and the court wishes to impose no separate penalty for one or more of those instances.

Use of Adjournment After a breach has been admitted or proved, the court may be uncertain whether the order has a viable future or not, particularly where the offender has not made recent contact with the relevant officer but argues that s/he is now resolved to complete the order. The court may opt to adjourn proceedings for a convenient period (*eg* four weeks) to give the offender the opportunity to demonstrate their new commitment. This procedure has the merit of keeping the prosecution before the court and the option, if the offender fails to comply, to proceed to revoke the order or (in the case of a Crown Court order) to remit the matter to the Crown Court (as outlined below). Some clerks or courts may discourage this form of delay, feeling that the matter should be resolved as quickly as possible, either by a penalty to mark the breach or by termination or by placing the issue before the Crown Court to adjudicate.

Power of Revocation If the order was imposed by a magistrates' court and the supervising court concludes that the order has ceased to be viable or should be terminated, the court:

> 'may revoke the order and deal with (the offender) for the offence in respect of which the order was made, in any manner in which it could deal with (the offender) if s/he had just been convicted by the court of the offence' (para. 3(1)(d)).

The court does not have the option simply to revoke without dealing with the offender afresh.

Crown Court Order: Power to Remit A magistrates' court has no power to revoke an order made by the Crown Court but 'may instead commit the offender to custody or release him/her on bail until s/he can be brought or appear before the Crown Court' (para. 3(3)). The magistrates may feel that in the circumstances the future of the order ought to be reviewed by the Crown Court though it would seem inappropriate for the matter to be referred to the Crown Court if the lower court feels that revocation is not a realistic option. There is nothing to prevent the relevant officer exercising discretion to allow the offender to continue working while the Crown Court hearing is awaited, though the offender should be aware that if the order is revoked (even if the total hours have been completed meantime) this effort may count only in mitigation and that the possibility of being re-sentenced remains.

Powers of the Crown Court

Where an offender has been remitted to the Crown Court and 'it is proved to the satisfaction of the court that s/he failed to comply with any of the requirements of the relevant order, that court may deal with (the offender) in respect of the failure in any one of the following ways' (para. 4(1)):

(a)   impose a fine not exceeding £1,000;

(b)   make a community service order, for a number of hours not exceeding 60 in the aggregate (para. 6(3)(a));

(c)   'revoke the order and deal with the offender for the offence in respect of which the order was made, in any manner in which it could deal with him/her if s/he had just been convicted by or before the court of the offence' (para. 4(1)(d)).

The Crown Court has complete discretion and is not tied by the magistrates' decision not to allow the order to continue.

Community Service as a Penalty for Breach

The power to impose community service as a penalty in this context differs somewhat from the use of CS as a community order.

Length Though there is a ceiling of 60 hours in aggregate, there is no specified minimum as the usual 40 hours minimum does not apply. A further limitation is set by para. 6(3)(b) which specifies that the order imposed under paras. 3(1) or 4(1):

'shall not be such that the total number of hours under both orders (*ie* the existing community order and the proposed 'penalty' order) exceeds the maximum specified in PCCA 1973 s14(1A)' (words in brackets mine).

Section 14(1A) refers to the maximum permissible aggregate of 240 hours (or 100 hours where the breached order is a combination order). Schedule 2 does not make clear whether the relevant consideration in gauging that maximum should be the aggregate number of hours specified in the orders or the combined number of hours that the offender will now be required to work, discounting any hours of the existing community order which have already been performed. The wording of para. 6(3)(b) appears to limit the aggregate to 240/100 hours irrespective of any hours already worked but such an interpretation would clearly limit the court's power to order a further period of community service where the offender is already subject to a long order and has not yet worked for a significant number of hours. Any order made may be imposed to run consecutively or concurrently to the original order and the court should clarify which is intended.

Procedural Requirements A pre-sentence report is not required, as it would be if the court was imposing CS as a community sentence but the court is nevertheless obliged to consider the offender's suitability and to hear from a probation officer or social worker ('if the court thinks it necessary'). This is because of the provisions of para. 6(4):

Section 14(2) of PCCA 1973 and so far as applicable:

(a)   the following provisions of that Act relating to community service orders; and

(b)   the provisions of this Schedule so far as so relating,

shall have effect in relation to a community service order under paragraph 3(1)(b) or 4(1)(b) above as they have effect in relation to a community service order in respect of an offender.

PCCA 1973 s14(3) also requires that the offender must consent to the making of a community service order and so consent must be secured in this context.

Enforcement Broadly speaking, a community service order imposed as a breach penalty is regulated and enforced in the same way as a CSO imposed as a sentence, by reason of para. 6(4)(b) cited above. Thus powers of amendment and revocation without re-sentence are clear, as are powers to deal with breach by the imposition of a fine or a further CSO. Paragraph 6(4)(b) is however qualified somewhat opaquely by para. 6(5):

Where the provisions of this Schedule have effect as mentioned in sub-paragraph (4) above, the powers conferred by those provisions to deal with the offender for the offence in respect of which the community service order was made shall be construed as powers to deal with the offender for the failure to comply with the requirements of the relevant order in respect of which the community service order was made.

Power to deal with the offender 'for the offence' arises in two instances: in breach proceedings where the order is terminated and in revocation proceedings where the court does not wish simply to revoke the order. The application of the sub-paragraph in these instances can be posed in the following hypothetical example:

An offender is initially sentenced to a community service order for 150 hours for affray. He breaches that order and is required to work a further 40 hours CS consecutive. He completes the initial 150 hours and then either breaches the subsequent order or is unable to complete those hours because of his changed circumstances. Thirty eight hours remain outstanding.

The sub-paragraph appears to convey that he should be treated in either breach or revocation proceedings as in breach of the initial order of 150 hours and thus stands to be dealt with for the affray offence, albeit that the initial sentence has been completed. His degree of compliance would be taken into account in the course of re-sentencing (see immediately below).

Re-Sentencing following Revocation

Because re-sentencing powers can also be exercised following a successful application for revocation, this somewhat complex issue is detailed separately in Chapter 8. In deciding how to deal with the offender, the court:

(a)   shall take into account the extent to which the offender has complied with the requirements of the relevant order; and

(b)   may assume, in the case of an offender who has wilfully and persistently failed to comply with those requirements, that s/he has refused to give his consent to a community sentence which has been proposed by the court and requires that consent (paras. 3(2) and 3(2)).

The provision in (b) links to CJA 1991 s1(3) which empowers a court to impose a custodial sentence for an offence which would not otherwise qualify for custody on grounds of seriousness if the offender refuses to give consent to a proposed community sentence requiring consent. The offender's non-co-operation permits (but does not oblige) the court to deem that the offender has refused consent, thus paving the way to a custodial sentence for the original offence, even though the 'so serious' threshold requirement has not been met.

Applications for Revocation

An application to revoke a community service order will be appropriate in the following circumstances. In each instance, the essential criterion for the court to consider is whether revocation 'would be in the interests of justice':

Changed Circumstances

The offender's present circumstances may render the order no longer viable or appropriate because of the prolonged or indefinite nature of their new situation. This will most commonly arise as a result of:

(a)   illness, accident or disability which renders the offender unfit for CS;

(b)   long-term employment or training commitments that leave no realistic capacity to undertake CS;

(c)   long-term family commitments which are sufficiently time-consuming to leave no realistic capacity to undertake CS.

An example combining both (b) and (c) would be an offender who is in full-time employment Monday to Friday and whose dependent child (ren) stay with them each weekend.

Conviction of a Further Offence

Though committing a further offence during the course of the order does not constitute a failure to comply with requirements, conviction of a further offence may provide appropriate grounds for a revocation application, primarily where a custodial sentence has been imposed for that offence. The main consideration will be the length of the custodial term and the portion of that sentence which will be spent in actual custody, the demands of any statutory early release licence or supervision which the offender will face on release and the offender's resettlement plans. The relevant officer will need to judge whether it is appropriate for the order to remain in temporary abeyance while the offender is not at liberty, to be resumed on release, or should be terminated. The offender may also have a view on the issue and may wish to be released from custody without the burden of resuming a continuing commitment of this nature. An application may be possible (and certainly convenient) on the same occasion that the custodial sentence is imposed or may need to be made subsequently.

Application Procedure

Application can be made by either the relevant officer or the offender in two instances:

(a) at any stage during the order to a magistrates' court acting for the specified PSA (the supervising court) (para. 7(1));

(b) to a magistrates' court other than the supervising court if the offender is convicted of a further offence by that other court and a custodial sentence is imposed (para. 9(1)). Though para. 9 does not specify the point at which an application should be made, the clear implication is that this will be appropriate on the occasion that the custodial sentence is passed. There seems nothing explicit to prohibit a subsequent application, if that opportunity is missed, other than the fact that para. 9 is silent as to how the offender is to be brought before the court, but at that later stage it will be altogether more appropriate and straightforward to make application to the supervising court.

If the application is made 'on the spot' in immediate response to the imposition of a custodial sentence, the application will normally be presented orally and, if the applicant is the relevant officer (or the court duty officer acting on their behalf), there is clearly no need to summon the offender who is already before the court. Alternatively, if a pre-sentence report is prepared for the new sentencing occasion, the writer may opt to address the question of revocation in the report, after consultation with the relevant officer. If this is felt to be undesirable, pre-judging the outcome of the case, an accompanying letter from the relevant officer to the clerk can indicate a wish to make application for revocation in the event of a custodial sentence being passed, which the clerk can then draw to the court's attention in the event that such a sentence is imposed.

In other instances, where application is made to the supervising court and the applicant is the relevant officer, the provisions of para. 7(7) apply:

Where a magistrates' court proposes to exercise its powers under this paragraph otherwise than on the application of the offender it shall summon him or her to appear before the court and, if s/he does not appear in answer to the summons, may issue a warrant for his or her arrest.

A summons is sought in the normal manner (*not* by laying an information) (see page 23) using Form 92M specified by MC(CJA 1991)(MA)R 1992. There is no power to seek a warrant (Form 92N) in the first instance and in circumstances where a warrant would appear necessary, the appropriate action would probably be a prosecution for breach (*eg* for failure to notify change of address) rather than a revocation application. If the application is prompted by the offender's conviction of a further offence resulting in a custodial sentence, a *production order* will need to be obtained by arrangement with the Crown Prosecution Service so that the offender can be brought to court from the prison establishment in which they are serving sentence.

Application by the Offender Schedule 2 does not give any indication of the circumstances in which application is more appropriately made by the offender. Practice guidelines in some areas suggest that if the offender is seeking to establish that their changed circumstances render their order no longer viable, the application should more properly be made by them, seeking the assistance of the clerk's office or the help of their solicitor. The relevant officer may take the view that it is valuable for the offender to assert their legal rights in this respect. If the offender makes application there is clearly no need or requirement for a summons to be issued. The court is very likely to seek the advice of the relevant officer both in respect of the merits of the application and the progress of the order to date. No application may be made by the offender under para. 7(1) while an appeal against the order is pending (para. 7(8)).

Considering an Application based on Changed Circumstances

If the application is made by the relevant officer to the supervising court, the court will expect an oral or written report outlining the progress of the order, including the number of hours performed, and the change of circumstances which appear to make the order unworkable. An offender who wishes to avoid exposure to re-sentencing may seek to persuade the court that their circumstances now permit the continuance and completion of the order. The court may thus opt to adjourn proceedings for a suitable period (*eg* four weeks) to allow the offender a further opportunity to demonstrate their preparedness to comply. Adjournment may be simple adjournment, without a remand on bail, if the offender has answered to summons.

If the court concludes that revocation would be in the interests of justice (*ie* the order has no viable future and should be terminated), the powers of the court depend on whether the community service order was imposed by the Crown Court or a magistrates' court. The supervising court may only revoke a magistrates' court order but in these circumstances has a choice of whether simply to revoke the order or to revoke and deal with the offender afresh for the original offence (para. 7(2)(a)).

The former option may be chosen where the hours specified in the order have been substantially completed or the offender's changed circumstances and/or the lapse of time since the original offence and their absence of convictions in the interim persuade the court that re-sentencing would not be in the interests of justice. This is a matter on which the defence will doubtless seek to address the court. In the majority of instances, especially where only a low percentage of the hours have been completed, the court will opt to revoke and deal afresh. The question will then arise whether a fresh pre-sentence report is required prior to re-sentencing.

If the order was imposed by the Crown Court, the supervising court must remit the matter to be considered by the Crown Court (para. 7(2)(b)). The question of revocation and re-sentence is addressed more fully in Chapter 8.

Revocation or Breach Proceedings?

In some instances there may be doubt in the relevant officer's mind whether application should be made in revocation proceedings or a prosecution initiated in breach proceedings. This dilemma is illustrated by *R v Jackson* (1984) 6 Cr App R(S) 202. The offender, aged 19, made a good start to her community service order (imposed in May by the Crown Court) but began to absent herself claiming various medical problems which were in the main covered by medical certificates. When she was interviewed in December by the relevant officer after a sustained period of absence, having completed 41 hours of a 180 hour order, she indicated that she was now employed at a turf accountant's office for six days a week and that she was not prepared to work for CS on her only day off. The relevant officer initiated revocation proceedings and when the matter eventually came before the Crown Court the order was revoked and a custodial sentence was imposed in its place. On her appeal against that re-sentence, the Court of Appeal considered it quite plain that the Crown Court judge did not accept that these excuses were put forward genuinely by this defendant, but noted that the judge 'had only had the benefit of a written report from the relevant officer'.

> 'It seems to us in retrospect that it would have been a great deal better had steps been taken, if necessary by way of adjournment, to put this matter on a proper evidential basis before the court was invited to exercise its very wide powers which undoubtedly exist (in revocation proceedings). The result is that what happened may very well have amounted to injustice to this defendant'.

Recognising the period that she had already spent in custody, the Court of Appeal quashed the custodial sentence and substituted a conditional discharge.

Breach proceedings offer a clear procedure for determining whether there has been a failure to comply and, although revocation can follow in both breach and revocation proceedings, the court may take a different view of whether and how to re-sentence the offender, if their response to the order is tested 'on a proper evidential basis' in breach proceedings. If the outcome is that a breach is not established, it would still be open either to the relevant officer or to the offender to apply for revocation as in the interests of justice in the light of the changed circumstances.

4.
COMBINATION ORDERS

Though designated as a single community order by CJA 1991 s6(4)(c) and s11, the combination order blends familiar elements of probation supervision and community service work. The Act is frustratingly lacking in detailed reference to the combination order in its own right, treating the order essentially as two separate legal entities, and thus generates substantial ambiguity in enforcement proceedings. Though reference should be made to the Chapters outlining the separate elements of the order, the following considerations are specific to the combination order.

Jurisdiction

The order specifies only one petty sessions area. It is not possible for the two elements to be under the jurisdiction of different PSAs.

Responsible Officer

CJA 1991 s15(3) does not identify who is to be regarded as the 'responsible officer' for enforcement purposes and instead recognises the function of the 'relevant officer' for CS purposes and the supervising officer for probation supervision purposes. The *National Standard* (1994, para. 7) is clear that:

> 'one probation officer should be identified as the supervising officer and given overall responsibility for a combination order'.

This is commonly the probation officer supervising the probation element, though this is a matter for local discretion. While the *National Standard* (1994, para. 12) asserts that:

> 'The decision on whether to institute breach proceedings should be taken by the supervising probation officer',

who should co-ordinate decision-making in the management of the order, it does not follow that enforcement proceedings should always and necessarily be in the name of that officer. Thus an application to amend the CS element by extending the period for completion beyond 12 months (sch 2 para. 15) could be sought by the relevant officer responsible for CS management. For the purposes of most proceedings, however, it is clearly sensible for the overall supervisor to take direct responsibility. Para. 12 goes on to state that 'one officer should be nominated to handle breach proceedings, including proving the breach and advising the court on possible future action'.

Enforcement Proceedings

The generic provisions of CJA 1991 sch 2 do not specifically designate the combination order as a 'relevant order' but instead specify (para. 1(2)):

> ...this schedule shall apply in relation to combination orders:
>
> (a)   in so far as they impose (a requirement of probation supervision), as if they were probation orders; and

(b) in so far as they impose (a requirement of community service work) as if they were community service orders.

The most crucial uncertainty arising from this dualism is whether it is possible for a court to revoke one element of the order while leaving the other intact, either in response to a revocation application, or in breach proceedings or even subsequent to a custodial sentence imposed for a further offence. The provisions of sch 2 para. 1(2) appear to empower such a split and Ward and Ward (1993, p72) go so far as to question whether it is possible for the court to revoke the whole order, even though they point out that in revocation proceedings initiated by the offender or responsible officer this could 'lead to the absurdity of two separate applications, with two separate summonses'. The logic of the combination order strongly suggests that the order should be regarded as an indivisible entity. Though simple revocation of one element without re-sentence would seem straightforward (*eg* where the offender has worked almost all of their community service hours but changed circumstances now prevent completion), clear problems would be presented in dealing with the offender afresh upon revocation of only one element of the order. On what basis is the court to assess what sentence is commensurate for the original offence when a part of the original sentence for that offence remains in force? Take a combination order with a CS element of 100 hours and two years probation supervision, where the offender's changed circumstances prevent further work after completion of only 20 hours and revocation is sought of only the CS element four months after the order was imposed. It is difficult to see how the court can readily assign a sentencing weight to the CS element of the order in deciding how to deal with the offender afresh in that limited respect. It seems far preferable for the court to review the order as a whole.

Though of no legal authority, the *National Standard* (1994) is clear that the combination order 'is a separate, single and integrated order of the court' (para. 2) and, in consequence (para. 15):

> 'If, following breach action, the court wishes to re-sentence the offender to either a probation order or a CSO, it must first revoke the combination order as a whole'.

Pending authoritative determination of this issue, it seems advisable to assume that the combination order may be revoked as a whole and upon single application, and this is reinforced by the form of MC(F)R 1981 Form 92P for use in 'revocation of probation, community service or combination order'. As a consequence, in all applications and prosecutions where the prospect of revocation arises, the responsible officer should proceed on the basis that partial revocation is not appropriate, even if technically permissible.

Amendment of the Order

Change of Residence In the light of the sole jurisdiction for judicial oversight of the order, it follows that an amendment to substitute another PSA will convey responsibility for the whole order to the new area. A complication arises if the offender is moving to Northern Ireland where the combination order does not exist. In this instance it seems appropriate to initiate revocation proceedings to revoke the order as a whole, leaving the court power to deal with the offender afresh, imposing either a probation order or community service order, specifying the petty sessions district in which the offender will now reside (in accordance with sch 3 paras. 2 and 4). If the offender stands convicted of two or more offences, it would be possible for the court to impose both a probation order and a community service order in place of the single combination order. If the court considers that it is empowered to revoke one element only of the order without re-sentence then this would allow the surviving element to be transferred.

Extension of CS If the offender does not complete their CS hours within the normal period of 12 months, application may be made under sch 2 para. 15 to extend the period for completion. Given the lower maximum of hours which may be imposed as the CS element of a combination order, the need for extension will arise only infrequently but the effect may be, unusually, that the CS element continues beyond the completion of the probation supervision element, if that is of 12 months duration.

Amendment of Requirements As the probation supervision element of the order may contain such additional requirements as may be included in a probation order, application may be made for such requirements to be cancelled, inserted or varied in the normal way.

Breach of the Order

Penalty Powers of the Court While it seems clear that a failure to comply with a requirement under either element constitutes a breach of the order as a whole, the powers of the court if the order is allowed to continue would appear to depend on which element has been breached. In practice the only significant difference is in respect of offenders under 21 for whom the court has the additional power to make an attendance centre order only where the relevant order is a probation order (or, in this instance, the breached element is that of probation supervision). Note also that where the court imposes additional community service hours as a penalty for breach the aggregate number of hours under both the CS element of the order and the additional hours should not exceed the lower maximum of 100 hours (sch 2 para. 1(3)) (see page 53).

Reporting to the Court 'Any report to the court in enforcement proceedings should address the offender's progress under both parts of the order' (*National Standard*, 1994 para. 15).

Revocation of the Order

The general issue of revocation is addressed above under 'Enforcement Proceedings'.

Early Termination for Good Progress If the provisions of sch 2 are interpreted to allow revocation of a single element of the order then there would appear to be nothing in law to prevent an application to revoke the probation element on grounds of good progress and satisfactory response. If the order can only be revoked as a whole then such an application would not be well founded while the CS element remains uncompleted as sch 2 paras. 7(3) and 8(3) do not provide for simple revocation without re-sentence in such circumstances. In any event, the *National Standard* (1994, para. 10) asserts that:

> 'Early termination... may be considered only after completion of the CS element of the order and then in accordance with the criteria for early termination of probation orders'.

5.
SUPERVISION ORDERS

Introduced by the Children and Young Persons Act 1969 s7(7) as a distinctive form of statutory provision for juveniles, the supervision order was designated as a 'community order' by CJA 1991 s6(4)(e). The 1969 Act nevertheless remains the governing statute for enforcement purposes.

Requirements of the Order

A supervision order is broadly defined as an order placing the offender under the supervision of a local authority designated by the order or of a probation officer (CYPA 1969 s11). This provision for the 'standard' order is supplemented by MC(C&YP)R 1992 r29(3) which permits either or both of the following requirements to be set out in the schedule of the standard order:

(a) That s/he shall inform the supervisor at once of any change of his/her residence or employment.

(b) That s/he shall keep in touch with the supervisor in accordance with such instructions as may from time to time be given by the supervisor and, in particular, that s/he shall, if the supervisor so requires, receive visits from the supervisor at his/her home.

Note that inclusion of (b) will require the offender to receive home visits, a requirement that is no longer stipulated in the 'standard' probation order.

Additional Requirements

The provisions of the 1969 Act empowering a court to include additional requirements are complex and for framing purposes reference should be made to the statute. Broadly, the Act permits the following:

s12 To comply with any directions from the supervisor requiring him/her to:

- live at a specified place(s) for specified periods; and/or

- present him/herself to a specified person at a specified place(s) on specified day(s); and/or

- participate in specified activities on a specified day(s), for up to 90 days (s12(2));

- to reside with a named individual (s12(1)).

s12A   To undertake any of the requirements that can be directed by the supervisor under s12(2) for up to 90 days (s 12A(3)(a)). (Where the court imposes a requirement of specified activities under s12A(3)(a) in place of a custodial sentence which it would otherwise have imposed, it should state this in open court and certify this in the order (s12D). This allows the court to re-sentence for the original offence in the event of a breach of the requirements – see below page 66).

To remain for specified periods (not exceeding 10 hours) between 6 pm and 6 am at a specified place or places, for not more than 30 days (s12A(3)(b)).

To refrain from participating in specified activities, either on specified days within the order or for the whole or a specified portion of the order (s12A(3)(c)).

s12AA To live for a specified period, not exceeding six months, in local authority accommodation, provided a number of pre-conditions are satisfied.

s12B To receive treatment for his/her mental condition, either as a resident or non-resident patient or under the direction of a specified medical practitioner.

s12C To comply with arrangements for his/her education as may be made by his/her parent.

In addition to these specific powers, CYPA 1969 s18(2)(b) enables a court to include 'such prescribed provisions as the court considers appropriate for facilitating the performance of' supervisory functions but if a requirement cannot be drafted within the specific provisions for additional requirements, it is probably unwise to resort to this somewhat open-ended provision. By far the most frequently used additional requirements specify activities to be undertaken under s12(2) or s12A(3)(a).

Jurisdiction

The order names the petty sessions area in which it appears to the court making the order that the supervised person will live (CYPA 1969 s18(2)(a)). Jurisdiction for enforcement purposes lies with 'the relevant court' (s15(1) and (3)) which means either a youth court or a magistrates' court acting for the PSA specified in the order, depending on whether the supervised person has attained the age of 18 or not at the time when the application is sought (s15(11) and s16(11)). If the supervised person attains the age of 18 while an application is pending, a youth court is still able to deal with the application (s16(11)).

The provisions of s15, supplemented by s16, apply a composite approach to variation, breach and discharge of supervision orders.

Except in a number of specified instances permitted under s16(5) (outlined below under the relevant headings), a court cannot make an order for variation, breach or discharge under s15 unless the supervised person is before the court (s16(1)). In cases where the supervised person makes application for variation or discharge this is clearly not a problem but, if the supervisor makes an application, the options to secure attendance are:

(a) for the supervisor to bring the supervised person before the court (*ie* by securing their co-operation to attend voluntarily) (s16(1)); or

(b) by issue of a summons (s16(2)); or

(c) if satisfied on oath that a summons cannot be served or if the supervised person fails to answer to summons, a justice may issue a warrant to secure attendance.

The form of summons in respect of a supervision order is specified by MC(C&YP)R 1992 sch 2 Form 4; Form 5 is the related summons for attendance of the juvenile's parent or guardian where they are required to attend (*ie* where the juvenile is aged under 16 or the court requests attendance in respect of an older juvenile).

Variation of the Order

CYPA 1969 s15

(1) If while a supervision order is in force in respect of a supervised person it appears to a relevant court, on the application of the supervisor or the supervised person, that it is appropriate to make an order under this subsection, the court may make an order... varying the supervision order:

(a) by cancelling any requirement included in it in pursuance of section 12,12A, 12AA, 12B, 12C or 18(2)(b) of this Act; or

(b) by inserting in it (either in addition to or in substitution for any of its provisions) any provision which could have been included in the order if the court had then had power to make it and were exercising the power.

(2) The powers of variation conferred by subsection (1) above do not include power:

(a) to insert in the supervision order, after the expiration of three months beginning with the date when the order was originally made, a requirement in pursuance of section 12B(1) of this Act, unless it is in substitution for such a requirement already included in the order; or

(b) to insert in the supervision order a requirement in pursuance of section 12A(3)(b) of this Act in respect of any day which falls outside the period three months beginning with the date when the order was originally made.

These provisions are both wide and somewhat complex and are supplemented further by related provisions in s16, including the following general 'care or control' caveat for the youth court:

CYPA 1969 s16(6)(a)

A youth court shall not exercise its powers under subsection (1) of the preceding section to make an order inserting in a supervision order a requirement authorised by section 12, 12A, 12AA, 12B or 12C of this Act or varying or cancelling such a requirement except in a case where the court is satisfied that the supervised person either is unlikely to receive the care or control he needs unless the court makes the order or is likely to receive it notwithstanding the order.

The following specific pointers attempt to summarise the options:

• The section does not make specific provision to amend the order by substituting a new petty sessions area where the offender changes address. This amendment can nevertheless be sought by use of the general power of substitution contained in s15(1)(b).

• Because the court can insert 'any provisions which could have been included in the order if the court then had power to make it and were exercising that power' (s15(1)(b)), the relevant consideration is the age of the offender at the time of the proposed variation. This will, for instance, affect whether it should be the offender or the offender's parents who should give any required consent to the proposed requirement (*eg* to a requirement under s12A(3)).

• The terms of s15(1)(b) allow the overall length of the supervision order to be reduced but not increased.

• A requirement of treatment for mental condition under s12B can be added to an order only within three months of the making of the order, unless it is in place of an existing requirement under that section (s15(2)(a)).

• Where the supervised person has attained the age of 14, a s12B requirement of treatment for mental condition cannot be inserted (or varied in any way other than by simple removal or reduction of the duration of the requirement) unless the supervised person consents (s16(7)).

• An additional requirement of 'night restriction' under s12A(3)(b) cannot specify a day which falls outside the first three months of the order's life (s15(2)(b)).

• Note that s15 allows a supervision order to be varied by the insertion of additional requirements without reference to the provisions of CJA 1991 s6(2) which require a court making a community sentence to impose restrictions on liberty commensurate with the seriousness of the offence(s). If the original order was deemed to impose restrictions appropriate to the seriousness, on what basis can additional restrictions be inserted? As with amendment of a probation order, where the same issue arises, the only logical interpretation would seem to be that if the restrictions contained in the original order fell below the commensurability ceiling, in the light of the offender's 'suitability', but the offender's personal circumstances have changed, the offender could now be suitable for further requirements which do not exceed that ceiling.

Supervisor's Duty to Seek Variation

A supervisor is under a duty to seek variation in two instances. First, as a general provision, a probation officer supervising a supervision order is required by the Probation Rules 1984 to make an application where it appears that 'an application can properly be made' (r39(4)), subject to the provision of r39(3) (see page 29). Secondly, in very specific circumstances, where a supervised person is subject to a requirement of treatment for mental condition under s12B and the medical practitioner responsible for that treatment is of the opinion:

(i)   that treatment should be continued beyond the period specified in the order; or

(ii)   that the supervised person needs different treatment; or

(iii)   that the supervised person is not susceptible to treatment; or

(iv)   that the supervised person does not require further treatment,

the practitioner should report this in writing to the supervisor who must then refer the matter to the relevant court seeking an appropriate variation (s15(9) and (10)).

Procedure

Where the supervised person makes the application, their attendance at court will clearly not be a problem but, if the supervisor makes application, the supervised person's attendance must be secured (and also their parents' where necessary) as outlined above (in the section on 'Jurisdiction'). These provisions permit the relatively draconian use of a warrant to bring the person before the court though the justification for resorting to this to secure attendance for a variation hearing is questionable, particularly if the offender's consent is required before the variation can proceed.

Remand to LAA: If the relevant court is a youth court which is considering whether to exercise its powers of variation (or discharge), the court may remand the supervised person to local authority accommodation in the interim, provided that one of two conditions is satisfied (s16(4)); either:

(a)   a warrant had been issued to bring the person before the court; or

(b)   the court considers that such a remand will enable information to be obtained which is likely to assist the court in deciding whether and how to exercise its powers.

The exceptions permitted by s16(5) allow a court to vary an order in the supervised person's absence in the following respects:

(a)   cancelling an additional requirement;

(b)   reducing the duration of the order or of any additional requirement;

(c)   changing the supervisor (for example, from a local authority to a probation officer);

(d)   altering the name of the local authority and/or petty sessions area specified in the order.

The form for an order varying or discharging a supervision order is prescribed by MC(C&YP)R 1992 sch 2 Form 39.

Appeal: The supervised person may appeal to the Crown Court against a variation order except one which the court is empowered to make in the supervised person's absence or a variation adding a requirement of mental treatment to which the supervised person, being aged 14 or more, consented.

Discharge of the Order

Apart from power to discharge the order in breach proceedings, outlined below, s15 also makes provision for early termination of a supervision order in discharge proceedings.

CYPA 1969 s15

(1) If while a supervision order is in force in respect of a supervised person, it appears to a relevant court, on the application of the supervisor or the supervised person, that it is appropriate to make an order under this subsection, the court may make an order discharging the supervision order...

This power is exercisable even if the supervision order was imposed by the Crown Court, which cannot reserve power of discharge to itself.

An obvious use of this power would be upon application for early termination for good progress, as advocated by the *National Standard* (1994, para. 24):

'Early termination of an order should be considered where the offender has made good progress in achieving the objectives set out for the order and where there is not considered to be a significant risk of re-offending and/or of serious harm to the public'.

Note that there is no specific statutory provision for a supervision order to be discharged following the supervised person's conviction of a further offence, even if a custodial sentence or incompatible community order (*eg* a probation order) has been imposed for the fresh offence and even upon conviction or sentence by the Crown Court. In the event that the new sentence appears to make the supervision order redundant, it is open to the supervisor or the supervised person to apply to the relevant court for discharge under s15(1), either 'on the spot' (if the further sentence is imposed by that court) or subsequently.

If application is made by the supervisor, the supervised person may be brought before the court by one of the means outlined above in the section on 'Jurisdiction', but s16(5)(a) allows a court to order discharge in the absence of the supervised person.

Remand to LAA: A youth court's power under s16(4) to remand the supervised person to local authority accommodation pending its decision is outlined above (page 62) in the context of Variation Procedure.

Moratorium after Dismissal: If the discharge application is dismissed, no further application for discharge can be made for three months from the date of dismissal unless the relevant court gives specific permission for an earlier application to proceed (s16(9)).

Appeal: The supervised person may appeal to the Crown Court against the dismissal of a discharge application (s16(8)(b)).

Breach of the Order

Grounds for Prosecution

The general grounds for breach action are that the supervised person 'has failed to comply with any requirement included in the supervision order' which could be lawfully imposed under the provisions of the 1969 Act (s15(3)). The court will need to be satisfied as follows:

(a) the supervision order is in force (or was so at the point when proceedings were initiated);

(b) the offender is the person subject to that order;

(c) the offender has failed to comply with a valid requirement of that order.

Unlike the provisions pertaining to other community orders, s15 does not specify that the failure should be 'without reasonable excuse'. It might thus appear at face value that 'reasonable excuse' for the default is only a relevant consideration in mitigation when determining how an established breach should be dealt with by the court. However, the courts are always reluctant to construe that Parliament intended to create an offence or, in this case, a punishable default, based on strict liability. In any case, a supervisor is highly unlikely to initiate breach proceedings if the supervised person has given an 'acceptable explanation' for their apparent failure. The *National Standard* (1994, para. 7), instructing the supervisor to seek an explanation, states:

> 'If the explanation is not considered acceptable, the incident must formally be recorded as an instance of failure to comply with a requirement of the order'.

The particular grounds on which a breach may be alleged are:

(a) failure to keep in touch with the supervisor in accordance with an instruction;

(b) failure to receive a notified visit at home from the supervisor;

(c) failure to notify the supervisor promptly of a change of address;

(d) failure to notify the supervisor promptly of a change of employment;

(e) failure to comply with any additional requirement specified in the order.

Breach action on grounds of unacceptable behaviour while fulfilling supervision require-ments, *eg* racist abuse or sexual harassment, is less clear-cut. Please refer to page 32 where the question of misbehaviour and non-compliance with instructions are more fully outlined.

Initiating Prosecution

The scope for non-judicial enforcement, outlined by the relevant *National Standard* (1994, paras. 26–29), mirror the provisions in respect of probation orders (see page 35). It is desirable that a parent or other adult should be present when the young person is being dealt with under any enforcement procedure.

Section 15 does not specify that the supervisor should lay an information, the normal way to initiate breach proceedings. Instead, the relevant court acts upon the application of the supervisor. No form of application is prescribed by MC(C&YP)R 1992 sch 2. A suggested form of application by means of a draft summons is included in this Chapter.

In all instances the supervised person is required to be present and their attendance (and also their parents', where necessary) is secured as outlined above (in the section on 'Jurisdiction').

Where the supervised person is arrested in pursuance of a warrant and cannot be brought before the court immediately, arrangements may be made for their detention in a place of safety for not more than 72 hours from time of arrest (s16(3)(a)). If not brought before the court within that period, the supervised person shall be brought before a justice, who has the following options:

(a) to release the supervised person forthwith (s16(3A)(a) which makes no provi-sion for the person to be bailed); or

(b) if the supervised person is under 18, remand him or her to local authority accommodation (s16(3A)(b)), provided by the authority named in the supervi-sion order (s16(3B));

(c) if the supervised person has attained the age of 18, s/he may be remanded either to a remand centre or, if no centre is available, to a prison (s16(3C)).

If the supervised person is brought before a youth court and that court is considering whether to make an order varying or discharging the supervision order under s15(1) powers, the supervised person may be remanded (or further remanded) to local authority accommodation, pending the outcome of proceedings, providing that one of two condi-tions is satisfied (s16(4)); either

(a) a warrant had been issued to bring the supervised person before the court; or

(b) the court considers that such a remand will enable information to be obtained which is likely to assist the court in deciding whether and how to exercise its powers.

Powers of the Court

If failure to comply is admitted or proved, the powers of the court depend on the age of the supervised person.

Age under 18 The court has the discretion under s15(1) either

(a) to discharge the order, or

(b) to vary the order (subject to the normal limitations on variation powers out-lined on page 61).

In both instances a youth court is required to heed the considerations of s16(6)(a) relating to the care and control of the supervised person (see page 61). Whether or not it exercises either of these powers, the court may also impose (s15(3)(a)):

(a)   a fine (not exceeding level 3, currently £1,000, or £250 for a child under 14); or

(b)   an attendance centre order (which becomes enforceable as if imposed under CJA 1982 s17: CYPA 1969 s16A(1)).

Note that the court may discharge the order *and* fine/impose an ACO, whereas in respect of community orders regulated by CJA 1991 sch 2, the court has to choose either to exercise penalty powers of fine/CSO or to revoke but cannot do both.

Upon discharging the order there is no general power when dealing with this age group to re-sentence for the original offence but scope to re-sentence arises in the specific instance of an order containing a requirement of specified activities under s12A(3)(a) where the court imposing that requirement specified under s12D that it was doing so instead of passing a custodial sentence (s15(4) and (6), detailed further below).

Age 18 or over In addition to the powers outlined above in respect of under 18s, a court exercising its power to discharge the order has a general power to impose any punishment, *other than YOI detention*, as if it then had power to try the supervised person for the original offence and had convicted them. Any fine thus imposed should not exceed £5,000 (level 5) (s15(5)(b)).

Breach of specified activities requirement with s12D statement: all ages In this special instance, where the offender has failed to comply with a requirement imposed under s12A(3)(a) (specified activities determined by the court), the court has a power of re-sentence, *including* power to impose a sentence of YOI detention, provided that the requirement was specifically imposed instead of a custodial sentence under s12D (s15(4) and (6)).

Note that the wording of s15(4) indicates that the breach proceedings must concern a failure to comply with the specified activities requirement rather than any other requirement within the order. It is unlikely, however, that the supervised person will have defaulted on another requirement while adhering to the specified activities expectations. The issue will probably only arise in practice if the supervised person has completed the specified activities requirement in full and subsequently defaults on the continuing order.

The court may make any order as if it then had power to try him or her for the original offence and had convicted them (s15(4)(a)). If the court has no jurisdiction to try the offender for that offence (*ie* where an adult magistrates' court is dealing with a supervision order imposed by a youth court for an offence triable only on indictment, in the case of an adult) its powers of re-sentence shall not exceed the powers of the court which does have that power and, additionally, shall not exceed a term of six months custody and a fine of £5,000 (s5(5)(a) and (c)).

Taking account of partial compliance: In all cases where a court deals with a breach under s15(3) or (4), whether discharging and re-sentencing or not, the court is required to 'take into account the extent to which the supervised person has complied with the requirements of the supervision order' (s15(8)).

Appeal: The supervised person may appeal to the Crown Court against any order made under s15(3) and (4), except an order for simple discharge or the cancellation or the reduction of a requirement, or a variation to which s/he gave any necessary consent.

BARCHESTER YOUTH COURT

Date :	1 November 1994
To (accused) :	Grace Ann AYRES **DoB :** 1.4.1978
Address :	19 Ladysmith Terrace, Barchester, Barsetshire

You are hereby summonsed to appear before Barchester Youth Court for the hearing of an application that you have failed to comply with a requirement of the supervision order made in your case.

Date of appearance :	18 November 1994
Time :	10.00 am
Court House address :	The Court House, Allington Road, Barchester, Barsetshire

Details of Order

Supervision Order (CYPA 1969 s7(7))

Court which made the Order :   Barchester Youth Court

Date of Order : 10.5.1994   **Duration of Order :** 12 months

Offence in respect of which Order made : Assault occasioning actual bodily harm

Petty Sessions Area specified in Order : Barchester

Local Authority specified in Order : Barchester County Council

Basis of application :   That you failed to receive a visit from the supervisor at your home on 20 October 1994, as required of you by instruction given to you by the supervisor on 12 October 1994.

Supervisor : Anthonia TROLLOPE, Social Worker

Address : County Offices, Cathedral Close, Barchester

Justices' Clerk/
Justice of the Peace

Summons for application alleging breach of Supervision Order

CYPA 1969 s15

(3) If while a supervision order made under section 7(7) of this Act is in force in respect of a person it is proved to the satisfaction of a relevant court, on the application of the supervisor, that the supervised person has failed to comply with any requirement included in the supervision order in pursuance of section 12, 12A, 12AA, 12C or 18(2)(b) of this Act, the court:

(a) whether or not it also makes an order under subsection (1) above, may order him or her to pay a fine of an amount not exceeding £1,000 or, subject to section 16A(1) of this Act, may make an attendance centre order in respect of him or her; or

(b) in the case of a person who has attained the age of 18, may (if it also discharges the supervision order) make an order imposing on him any punishment, other than a sentence of detention in a young offender institution, which it could have imposed on him or her if it:

(i) had then had power to try him or her for the offence in consequence of which the supervision order was made; and

(ii) had convicted him or her in the exercise of that power.

(4) If while a supervision order is in force in respect of a person it is proved to the court under subsection (3) above that the supervised person has failed to comply with any requirement included in the supervision order in pursuance of section 12A(3)(a) of this Act directing the supervised person to participate in specified activities, the court may, if it also discharges the supervision order, make an order imposing on him or her any sentence which it could have imposed on him if it:

(a) had then had power to try him or her for the offence in consequence of which the supervision order was made; and

(b) had convicted him or her in the exercise of that power.

(5) In a case falling within subsection (3)(b) or (4) above where the offence in question is of a kind which the court has no power to try, or has no power to try without appropriate consents, the sentence imposed by virtue of that provision:

(a) shall not exceed that which any court having power to try such an offence could have imposed in respect of it; and

(b) where the case falls within subsection (3)(b) above and the sentence is a fine, shall not in any event exceed £5,000; and

(c) where the case falls within subsection (4) above, shall not in any event exceed a custodial sentence for a term of six months and a fine of £5,000.

(6) A court may not make an order by virtue of subsection (4) above unless the court which made the supervision order made a statement under subsection (1) of section 12D of this Act; and for the purposes of this subsection a certificate under that section shall be evidence of the making of the statement to which it relates.

6.
ATTENDANCE CENTRE ORDERS

Subject to the availability of a centre for persons of the offender's age and gender, attendance centre orders may be imposed on young offenders aged under 21 in four instances:

(a)   as a community sentence (CJA 1991 s6(4)(f));

(b)   as a penalty for non-payment of a fine or other financial penalty where an adult could be committed to prison (CJA 1982 s17(1)(a));

(c)   as a penalty for breach of a supervision order (CYPA 1969 s15(3A));

(d)   as a penalty for breach of a probation order (CJA 1991 sch 2 paras. 3(1)(c) and 4(1)(c)).

In all these instances the enforcement of the order is governed by CJA 1982 ss 16–19, backed by the Attendance Centre Rules 1994 (currently in draft), replacing the 1958 Rules, and reinforced by a *National Standard* (1994) (currently in draft).

Requirements of the Order

The basic requirement of the order, specified by CJA 1982 s17(1), is for the offender:

'to attend at such centre to be specified in the order, for such number of hours as may be so specified'.

This is supplemented by ACR 1994 r10:

'Persons shall while attending at a centre behave in an orderly manner and shall obey any instruction given by the officer in charge or any member of staff'.

The order specifies the date and time of the first occasion of attendance 'and subsequently at such times as shall be fixed by the officer in charge of that centre'. The order does not specify a petty sessions area but judicial oversight is normally exercised by a magistrates' court acting for the petty sessions area in which the specified attendance centre is situated (CJA 1982 s18(3)(a) and (5), s19 (2)(a)). Jurisdiction may also be exercised for certain purposes by the court which made the order, including the Crown Court, as summarised in the Table below. Responsibility for enforcement rests with the officer in charge, though the offender has the right to seek variation or discharge of the order.

Court Making Order	Power of Variation and Breach	Power of Discharge
Crown Court	Court acting for PSA in which Centre is situated	(1) Court acting for PSA in which Centre is situated UNLESS power reserved by the Crown Court (2) Crown Court
Magistrates' Court	(1) Court acting for PSA in which Centre is situated, or (2) Court which made the order	

Variation of the Order

CJA 1982 s18

(5) An attendance centre order may, on the application of the offender or of the officer in charge of the relevant attendance centre, be varied by a magistrates' court acting for the petty sessions area in which the relevant attendance centre is situated; and an attendance centre order made by a magistrates' court may also be varied, on such an application, by that court.

(6) The power to vary an attendance centre order is a power by order:

(a) to vary the day or hour specified in the order for the offender's first attendance at the relevant attendance centre; or

(b) to substitute for the relevant attendance centre an attendance centre which the court is satisfied is reasonably accessible to the offender, having regard to his age, the means of access available to him and any other circumstances.

(7) Where an application is made under this section by the officer in charge of an attendance centre, the court may deal with it without summoning the offender.

Substituting Another Centre: This power is not confined to instances where the offender has changed or is about to change address but is exercisable in any circumstances where it would be more suitable for the offender to attend a different centre. The wording of an order varying an attendance centre order in this way is specified by MC(C&YP)R 1992 sch 2 form 26.

Changing Date/Time of First Attendance: This is a somewhat limited power exercisable at the commencement of the order. Thereafter, the officer in charge has a discretion when to require the offender's subsequent attendance and has a duty to inform the offender before s/he leaves the centre of the day and time of next attendance, both orally and in writing (ACR 1994 r5(2)). There is no power to vary the number of hours for which the offender is required to attend.

Breach of the Order

Non-Judicial Sanctions

ACR 1994 specify a number of sanctions which may be imposed either instead of or in addition to the initiation of formal breach proceedings:

(a) segregation from other offenders;

(b) undertaking an alternative task;

(c) being required to leave the centre for the remainder of the session;

(d) suspension from further attendance pending court appearance for breach.

When the breach is serious, the officer in charge should interview the offender and caution him or her as to their future conduct at the centre, before imposing the sanction (*National Standard*, para. 42).

ACR 1994 r11

11. (1) The officer in charge may at any time require any person committing a breach of these Rules to leave the centre.

(2) Where a person is so required to leave, he shall either:

    (a) be instructed in accordance with r5(2) as to his further attendance at the centre; or

    (b) be informed (both orally and in writing) that he is not required to attend at the centre again and that it is intended in respect of the said breach to take steps to bring him before a court under CJA 1982 s19(1).

12. (Where a person has been required to leave the centre, the subsequent period of that session shall not count towards their tally of hours).

13. Without prejudice to the generality of the last foregoing rule, the officer in charge or any member of the staff may deal with a person committing a breach of these rules in either or both of the following ways, that is to say:

    (a) by separating him from other persons attending at the centre;

    (b) by giving him an alternative form of occupation;

during the whole or any part of the period of attendance specified in the order then remaining uncompleted.

If the offender fails to attend without permission, a phone call should, where possible, be made to their home to find out the reason for absence. A warning letter should be sent both to the offender and also, in the case of under 16s, to their parents. A home visit may be made at the discretion of the officer in charge. Breach action must be initiated no later than the third consecutive absence, or earlier if the officer in charge is satisfied that the offender has no intention of obeying the sentence of the court. When unauthorised absences are not consecutive, the officer in charge can be more flexible but generally no more than four non-consecutive absence should be tolerated (para. 44).

Judicial Sanctions

CJA 1982 s19 provides that breach proceedings may be brought on two grounds:

    (a)   failure to attend in accordance with the order, including late arrival; or

    (b)   while attending, committing a breach of the rules which cannot be adequately dealt with under those rules. This essentially means either a failure to behave in an orderly manner or a failure to respond to instructions from staff.

Jurisdiction rests with a court acting for the petty sessions area in which the specified centre is situated or, in the case of an order made by a magistrates' court, a court acting for the same PSA as the court which made the order. Proceedings are initiated in the normal way by laying an information, using the format laid down by MC(C&YP)R 1992 sch 2 form 7. If the information is in writing and on oath, a justice may issue a warrant for the offender's arrest to bring him or her before the court.

If on the offender's appearance the breach is admitted or it is proved to the satisfaction of the court that s/he has failed without reasonable excuse to attend or has committed a breach of the rules, the powers of the court depend on whether the order was made by a magistrates' court or the Crown Court.

Magistrates' Court Order: The court may either (i) fine the offender up to maximum for a level 3 offence (currently £1,000 or £250 for an offender aged under 14) and allow the order to continue or (ii) revoke the order and deal with the offender afresh for the original offence (s 19(3)(a)). MC(C&YP)R 1992 sch 2 forms 27 and 28 specify the form of the orders made in these instances.

Crown Court Order: The court may either (i) fine the offender (as outlined above), allowing the order to continue, or (ii) remit the matter back to the Crown Court. If the latter course is chosen, the offender may be committed in custody or remanded on bail to appear at Crown Court (s 19(3)(b)). Where the Crown Court is satisfied that the breach has occurred, the court may revoke the order and deal with the offender afresh for the original offence (s 19(5)). Though the Crown Court is not expressly empowered to deal with the breach by fine, allowing the order to continue, this seems a valid option open to the court.

Re-Sentencing Powers: The court revoking the order may deal with the offender for the offence for which the order was made:

> 'in any manner in which it could have dealt with him for that offence if it had not made the order' (s 19(3)(a) and (5)).

This appears to mean that the offender should be dealt with on the basis of their age as it was when the order was imposed, subject to the powers and restrictions that applied at that time in that court.

The court is required under s19(5A)(a) to take into account the extent to which the offender has complied with the requirements of the order and can thus give credit for partial performance. In addition, the court may assume, 'in the case of an offender who has wilfully and persistently failed to comply' with their order, that s/he has refused to give consent 'to a community sentence which has been proposed by the court and requires that consent' (s 19(5A)(b)). An attendance centre order does not require consent but this provision empowers the court in such instances to impose a custodial sentence under CJA 1991 s1(3). This allows a custodial sentence to be imposed upon an offender who refuses consent to a community order, even though the offence would not otherwise attract a custodial sentence on grounds of seriousness. Custody is not inevitable in such circumstances, as the offender may well be suitable for and willing to consent to a different community order which the court is prepared to impose. In this context, 'persistently' means as a minimum that the offender breached the order on more than one occasion.

CJA 1982 s19

(1) Where an attendance centre order has been made and it appears on information to a justice acting for a relevant petty sessions area that the offender:

(a) has failed to attend in accordance with the order; or

(b) while attending has committed a breach of rules made under section 16(3) above which cannot be adequately dealt with under those rules,

the justice may issue a summons requiring the offender to appear at the place and time specified in the summons before a magistrates' court acting for the area or, if the information is in writing and on oath, may issue a warrant for the offender's arrest requiring him to be brought before such a court.

(2) For the purposes of this section a petty sessions area is a relevant petty sessions area in relation to attendance centre order:

    (a) if the attendance centre which the offender is required to attend by an order made by virtue of section 17(1) or 18(6)(b) above is situated in it; or

    (b) if the order was made by a magistrates' court acting for it.

(3) If it is proved to the satisfaction of the magistrates' court before which an offender appears or is brought under this section that he has failed without reasonable excuse to attend as mentioned in paragraph (1) of subsection (1) above or has committed such a breach of rules as is mentioned in paragraph (b) of that subsection, that court may, without prejudice to the continuation of the order, impose on him a fine not exceeding £1,000 or:

    (a) if the attendance centre order was made by a magistrates' court, may revoke it and deal with him, for the offence in respect of which the order was made, in any manner in which he could have been dealt with for that offence by the court which made the order if the order had not been made;

    (b) if the order was made by the Crown Court, may commit him in custody or release him on bail until he can be brought or appear before the Crown Court.

(3A) Section 18 of the Criminal Justice Act 1991 (fixing of fines) shall apply for the purposes of subsection (3) above as if the failure to attend or the breach of the rules were a summary offence punishable by a fine not exceeding level 3 on the standard scale; and a fine imposed under that subsection shall be deemed for the purposes of any enactment to be a sum adjudged to be paid by a conviction.

(4) A magistrates' court which deals with an offender's case under subsection (3)(b) above shall send to the Crown Court a certificate signed by a justice of the peace giving particulars of the offender's failure to attend or, as the case may be, the breach of the rules which he has committed, together with such other particulars of the case as may be desirable; and a certificate purporting to be so signed shall be admissible as evidence of the failure or the breach before the Crown Court.

(5) Where by virtue of subsection (3)(b) above the offender is brought or appears before the Crown Court and it is proved to the satisfaction of the Court that he has failed to attend as mentioned in paragraph (a) of subsection (1) above or has committed such a breach of rules as is mentioned in paragraph (b) of that subsection, that Court may revoke the attendance centre order and deal wth him, for the offence in respect of which the order was made, in any manner in which it could have dealt with him for that offence if it had not made the order.

(5A) In dealing with an offender under subsection (3)(a) or (5) above, the court concerned:

    (a) shall take into account the extent to which the offender has complied with the requirements of the attendance centre order; and

    (b) may assume, in the case of an offender who has wilfully and presistently failed to comply with those requirements, that he has refused to give his consent to a community sentence which has been proposed by the court and requires that consent.

(6) A person sentenced under subsection (3)(a) above for an offence may appeal to the Crown Court against the sentence.

(7) In proceedings before the Crown Court under this section, any question whether there has been a failure to attend or a breach of the rules shall be determined by the Court and not by the verdict of a jury.

Breach of ACO Imposed for Breach

If the attendance centre order was imposed for breach of either a probation order or a supervision order, the question arises as to the powers of the court where the offender fails to comply with the ACO and that order is revoked. What are the powers of the court revoking the order to address either the probation/supervision order or the offence for which that supervisory order was imposed?

In regard to an ACO imposed under CYPA 1969 s15(3)(a), s16A(2) of that Act specifies that CJA 1982 ss18 and 19 shall apply but as if the words 'for the offence in respect of which the order was made' and 'for that offence' were omitted from s19(3) and (5). This means that, on revocation, the offender may be dealt with in any manner in which s/he could have been dealt with by the court which made the order if the order had not been made. This thus gives the court power to deal with the breach of the supervision order afresh even if that order has meanwhile expired.

In regard to an ACO imposed under CJA 1991 sch 2, a similar issue has already been addressed in respect of a CSO imposed as a breach penalty (see page 51) but whereas sch 2 para. 6 makes specific provision for failure to comply with a CSO imposed in such circumstances, there is no equivalent provision in respect of an ACO made in such circumstances. Thus the powers of the court when dealing with a failure to comply with such an order are somewhat uncertain.

Discharge of the Order

CJA 1982 s18

(1) An attendance centre order may be discharged on an application made by the offender or the officer in charge of the relevant attendance centre.

(2) An application under subsection (1) above shall be made to one of the courts specified in subsection (3) below or to the Crown Court under subsection (4) below, and the discharge of such an order shall be by order of the court.

(3) Subject to subsection (4) below, the power to discharge an attendance centre order shall be exercised:

    (a) by a magistrates' court acting for the petty sessions area in which the relevant attendance centre is situated; or

    (b) by the court which made the order.

(4) Where the court which made the order is the Crown Court and there is included in the order a direction that the power to discharge the order is reserved to that court, the power shall be exercised by that court.

(4A) The power to discharge an attendance centre order includes power to deal with the offender, for the offence in respect of which the order was made, in any manner in which he could have been dealt with for that offence by the court which made the order if the order had not been made.

(7) Where an application is made under this section by the officer in charge of an attendance centre, the court may deal with it without summoning the offender.

This power would be appropriately used if the offender's state of health made him or her unsuitable for the demands of the sentence, or their employment demands now make attendance impossible, or if the offender moves to an area where a centre is not conveniently available for their age or gender group. It is not intended for use simply where the offender has made 'good progress' but is otherwise capable of completing the order in the normal way. The other instance in which a discharge application could be appropriate is upon the offender's conviction of a further offence (see below).

Note that a magistrates' court acting for the petty sessions area in which the centre is situated has the power to discharge an order made by the Crown Court, an advantage which does not normally apply to community orders, except where the Crown Court specifically reserved the power to discharge to itself (s 18(4)). Application to the Crown Court is direct (consult the Crown Court liaison probation officer) and not via a magistrates' court.

If a court opts to discharge the order, it now has power to deal with the offender for the offence for which the order was initially imposed (s 18(4A)), provided that the order was made on or after October 1 1992. Section 18 does not make explicit provision for bringing the offender before the court in such instances, yet clearly the offender's presence is required if the court proposes to re-sentence. Though an application by the officer in charge can be dealt with without summoning the offender (s 18(7)), and this would seem sensible if the court proposes merely to terminate the order without re-sentence, the court would certainly need to issue a summons to bring the offender before the court if re-sentencing is proposed.

A magistrates' court discharging a Crown Court order has no power to remit the matter back to the Crown Court for re-sentence, even if the order was made for an offence triable only on indictment. This appears to prevent an adult magistrates' court from re-sentencing the offender for such an offence. This problem is unlikely to arise in practice. The form of order used upon discharge of an attendance centre order is specified by MC(C&YP)R 1992 sch 2 form 25.

Further Conviction

There is no statutory provision for the discharge or revocation of an attendance centre order following conviction of a further offence, even if a custodial or other incompatible sentence is imposed for that offence or even upon conviction by the Crown Court. In these circumstances, it is open to the officer in charge or the offender to apply for discharge under the general provisions of s18, either 'on the spot' if an incompatible sentence is being imposed by a court having jurisdiction to discharge the order, or on subsequent application.

7.
CURFEW ORDERS

Introduced by CJA 1991 s12 and designated a community order by s6(4)(a), subject to the provisions of sch 2, the curfew order, backed by electronic monitoring arrangements, is expected to be tested in three pilot areas (Manchester, Norfolk and Reading) during 1995 and is therefore included in this guide, albeit in a somewhat rudimentary and tentative fashion.

Requirements of the Order

A curfew order requires the offender 'to remain, for periods specified in the order, at a place so specified' (s12(1)). The order 'may specify different places or different periods for different days', subject to two limitations (s12(2)):

(a)   periods specified must fall within six months of the making of the order;

(b)   periods shall be for a minimum of two hours and a maximum of 12 hours in any one day.

Additional Requirement of Electronic Monitoring

The order may include 'requirements for securing the electronic monitoring of the offender's whereabouts during the curfew periods specified in the order' (s13(1)), provided that the court has been notified by the Home Secretary that arrangements are available in the area where 'the place' is located and is satisfied that the necessary provision can be made under those arrangements (s13(2)). The prospects for curfew orders seem tied to electronic monitoring and it is expected that curfew orders will routinely carry such a requirement.

Jurisdiction

Though the order is not required to specify a petty sessions area, jurisdiction for enforcement purposes under CJA 1991 sch 2 lies with a court (the supervising court) acting for the PSA in which the place for the time being specified in the order is situated (para. 1(1)(b)).

Responsible Officer

For enforcement purposes, the responsible officer is the person responsible for monitoring the offender's whereabouts during curfew periods, as specified in the order (s12(4) and s15(3)(c)). Clarification is awaited whether this role will be undertaken by the probation service or by a private sector contractor.

Amendment of the Order

On Change of Residence

As with a probation order, where the supervising court is satisfied that the offender proposes to change or has changed residence to another PSA, the court may and on the application of the responsible officer shall amend the order by substituting a place in that other area for the place currently specified (para. 12(1) and (2)). However, if the order contains a requirement which, in the opinion of the court, cannot be complied with in the new area, the amendment shall not be made unless the court either cancels those requirements or substitutes other requirements which can be complied with within the proposed area (para. 12(3)). During the phase of experimental introduction of the order backed with electronic monitoring it is obvious that this form of amendment will not be possible if the offender is moving to live outside of the three trial areas and the alternative course will be to seek revocation of the order, with scope for re-sentencing. If the offender is moving address within the *same* PSA, amendment of the order by varying the specified 'place' will be required under para. 13 (below).

Variation of Requirements

Upon application by the responsible officer or the offender under sch 2 para. 13(1) the supervising court may:

(a)   cancel any requirements in the order;

(b)   insert an additional requirement in the order; or

(c)   substitute a new requirement for an existing requirement in the order.

However, the court may not vary the order by extending the periods of curfew beyond the end of six months from the date of the original order (para. 13(2)(b)). The relevant procedure is as pertains when seeking variation of a probation order. Imposition of an additional or substitute requirement sought by the responsible officer will require the offender's attendance and consent. No application may be made while an appeal against the order is pending. It remains to be seen whether short-term adjustments of curfew periods to fit any special commitments in the offender's life will need to be referred to the court for approval in the same way as variation of bail conditions of curfew, or can be negotiated with and approved at the discretion of the responsible officer.

Breach of the Order

The clear ground on which a breach may be alleged is:

(a)   failure to remain at the place specified during a period specified in the order.

At time of writing before the commencement of the pilot monitoring trials it is less clear whether there will be a further ground for prosecution:

(b)   failure to comply with electronic monitoring arrangements (*eg* failing to co-operate with the process of installation or interference with the equipment either as worn or installed in the offender's home).

A failure of this nature may well be associated with failure (a) but, if the equipment has been tampered with, the offender's absence from the specified place may be very difficult to prove and the evidence in respect of (b) may be more accessible. The statutory provisions do not make any specific provision for the offender's compliance with demands and efficient functioning of the equipment.

Breach procedures and powers are as outlined in respect of community service orders. It remains to be seen whether provision will be made in a *National Standard* for the first or second violation of curfew to be dealt with by formal warnings.

Revocation of the Order

A curfew order may be subject of a revocation application by the offender or the responsible officer or revocation at the instigation of the Crown Court in the same way as outlined elsewhere in respect of probation and community service orders. There is no provision for simple revocation on grounds of the offender's good progress and satisfactory response to the order. It is to be anticipated that the offender may seek revocation on grounds of their changed circumstances if they secure work which requires their absence from 'the specified place' to an extent which makes a curfew non-viable. Clearly such an application would need to be made promptly to ensure consideration prior to a violation leading to breach proceedings. If a breach prosecution is initiated in such circumstances, the offender would doubtless claim 'reasonable excuse'.

8.
REVOCATION AND RE-SENTENCE

This Chapter addresses issues in common for probation orders, community service orders, combination orders and curfew orders where the order is revoked under the generic provisions of CJA 1991 sch 2, either in breach or revocation proceedings, and the offender stands to be dealt with afresh for the original offence.

Powers of the Court in Revocation Proceedings

Powers of Magistrates' Courts

If, on the application of either the responsible officer or the offender, the court concludes that revocation would be in the interests of justice, the powers of the court depend on:

(a)   whether the community order was imposed by the Crown Court or a magistrates' court; and

(b)   whether the court is the supervising court or another magistrates' court.

Supervising Court dealing with a Magistrates' Court Order Under para. 7(2)(a) the court may:

(i)   revoke the order; or

(ii)   revoke the order and deal with the offender, for the offence in respect of which the order was made, in any manner in which it could deal with him or her if s/he had just been convicted by the court of the offence.

In dealing with an offender under sub-paragraph (2)(a)(ii) above, a magistrates' court shall take into account the extent to which the offender has complied with the requirements of the relevant order (para. 7(4)).

Supervising Court dealing with a Crown Court Order The court may remit the matter to the Crown Court, committing the offender to custody or releasing the offender on bail until s/he can be brought or appear before the Crown Court (para. 7(2)(b)). If the court agrees with the application, the court must, in effect, take this course.

Another Magistrates' Court In the limited circumstances to which para. 9 applies (*ie* upon conviction for a further offence and imposition of a custodial sentence), the court may:

(a)   if the order was made by a magistrates' court, revoke it; or

(b)   if the order was made by the Crown Court, commit the offender in custody, or release him or her on bail until s/he can be brought or appear before the Crown Court (para. 9(2)).

Note that the power in (a) is purely to revoke the order and does not extend to dealing with the offender afresh. If the court feels that the offender should be exposed to re-sentence for the original offence, it should decline the application, leaving it open for an application to be made to the supervising court.

Powers of the Crown Court

On Remittal from the Supervising Court Where the offender appears before the Crown Court under para. 7(2)(b) and it appears to be in the interests of justice to do so, the Court may:

(a)   revoke the order; or

(b)   revoke the order and deal with the offender, for the offence in respect of which the order was made, in any manner in which it could deal with him or her if s/he had just been convicted by the court of the offence (para. 8(2)).

In dealing with an offender under sub-paragraph (2)(b) above, the Crown Court shall take into account the extent to which the offender has complied with the requirements of the relevant order (para. 8(4)).

If the Crown Court declines to revoke, the order necessarily continues and any subsequent enforcement proceedings will need to be initiated afresh. If the offender seeks to avoid exposure to re-sentencing and persuades the Court that their circumstances now enable the continuance of the order, the Crown Court can either decline the application or may adjourn the matter to give the offender an opportunity to demonstrate their capacity to sustain the commitment satisfactorily.

On Remittal from Another Magistrates' Court under para. 9(2)(b)

Where by virtue of paragraph 9(2)(b) above an offender is brought or appears before the Crown Court and it appears to the Crown Court to be in the interests of justice to do so, having regard to circumstances which have arisen since the relevant order was made, the Crown Court may revoke the order (para. 10).

Note that this power does not include the option to deal with the offender afresh for the offence for which the order was made.

On Convicting the Offender of a Further Offence Separate from any process initiated on application leading to remittal to the Crown Court, the Crown Court has the power *of its own motion* to revoke the current order under para. 8(2)(a) or (b) (see above), where the offender is convicted of an offence before the Crown Court and it appears in the interests of justice to do so (para. 8(1)(a)). This power also arises where the offender is committed to the Crown Court for sentence for a further offence (para. 8(1)(b)). The power will be most appropriately used where a custodial sentence (or an incompatible community sentence) is imposed for the further offence and it appears necessary or desirable to terminate the existing order. The considerations mentioned in the context of an application in these circumstances (page 37) will apply here also. See also the discussion below. Note that the order must be in force at the point that the court acts to revoke it. It is not sufficient that the order was in force when the further offence was committed (*R v Cousin* (1994) 15 Cr App R(S) 516).

Though the Crown Court acts not upon formal application but upon its own initiative, it may be appropriate for either the Crown Court liaison officer on behalf of the responsible officer or the defence to invite the Court to consider this option and thus ensure that the opportunity of revocation is taken while the offender is before the Court, avoiding the inconvenience of a subsequent application to the supervising court.

The situation will frequently arise that an offender who is facing breach proceedings or a revocation application is simultaneously awaiting appearance before the Crown Court on further matters. If a guilty plea at Crown Court and a subsequent custodial sentence are anticipated, it may be more sensible to adjourn proceedings before the supervising court to await the outcome at the Crown Court, particularly to save trouble and expense in contested breach proceedings. The responsible officer can usefully brief the Crown Court liaison officer to ensure that the outstanding order is not overlooked at the Crown Court sentencing stage. Alternatively, if a pre-sentence report is prepared for the new sentencing occasion in the Crown Court, the writer may opt to address the possibility of revocation in the report, though this might be felt to be prematurely pre-judging the outcome of the case.

Relevant Age of the Offender

Note that the pertinent age of the offender for the purposes of determining the sentencing powers of the court dealing afresh with the offender is their age on the date when re-sentencing is undertaken, not their age when they were convicted of the original offence or were sentenced to the order now revoked. Thus if an offender was aged 19 when made subject to the community order but has now attained the age of 21, the court will now deal with him or her as an adult using powers pertaining to those aged 21 and over.

Custody for a Further Offence: Should the Community Order Continue?

Simply because the offender has received a custodial sentence for the further offence it does not necessarily follow that the community order should be revoked. It will be necessary to consider the length of the new custodial sentence, the time that the offender can expect to spend in custody, the duration of the community order, the offender's attitude towards the order, the demands of any statutory early release licence or supervision requirements, and the offender's re-settlement plans. In regard to probation orders the Court of Appeal has indicated that there may be merit in allowing the order to continue, albeit in temporary abeyance while the offender is not at liberty. In *R v Rowsell* (1988) 10 Cr App R(S) 411, the offender was subject to a probation order for three years for driving whilst disqualified and had committed a similar offence within a few weeks of the making of the order. He was sentenced to nine months imprisonment for the further offence but the probation order was allowed to continue. The Court of Appeal noted:

> 'In some cases it may be clear than an offender who has broken a probation order within a matter of days has shown that he has no intention of taking advantage of the help he has been offered, and it will be right to pass sentence for the original offence. In other cases where... the probation order has not had time to have effect, it may be correct to leave the order in being. In other cases it may be that so little will remain of the probation period after the offender's discharge from custody that it would be futile to leave the order in being. Each case will be different, and must be decided on its own facts' (per Ian Kennedy J).

More recently, in *R v Cawley* (1994) 15 Cr App R(S) 209 where the offender subject to a probation order was sentenced to nine months YOI for a further burglary offence, the Court of Appeal overturned the simultaneous revocation of the probation order noting that it seemed helpful and appropriate that the probation order should still be in place on his release (though the Court gave no acknowledgement that he would also be subject to separate statutory supervision under CJA 1991 s65).

If an order is revoked because the offender has been sentenced to custody for a further offence and an appeal against conviction of the further offence is successful, revocation of the order becomes automatically void and the order is thus reactivated (*R v Woodley* (1991) *The Times* 27 November).

Re-Sentencing to Custody

The question which will concern most defendants facing re-sentencing after revocation is whether they face the prospect of a custodial sentence for the original offence, either in addition to any custodial sentence imposed for a further offence or simply in place of the original community sentence. This is not always easy to anticipate but the following considerations are pertinent.

• The court must re-sentence in the light of the seriousness of the original offence. The fact that the offence was previously considered serious enough for a community sentence does not guarantee that the offence cannot now be considered sufficiently serious to justify a custodial sentence. As Lord Taylor CJ remarked in *R v Oliver and Little* [1993] 1 WLR 177, if a further offence is committed while a community sentence is in force the offender facing re-sentence:

> 'will have deprived himself of much of the mitigation such as good character, genuine remorse, isolated lapse and similar considerations which led the original court to pass a community sentence rather than a custodial sentence'.

• If the further offence was committed before the community order was imposed, the court should not normally re-sentence the offender for the original offence upon revocation, even if simple revocation is appropriate. Thus in *R v Cawley* (1994) 15 Cr App R(S) 209 where a probation order had been imposed following a further offence of burglary for which a custodial sentence was subsequently imposed, the Court of Appeal overturned the consecutive custodial sentence imposed in place of the probation order, stating:

> 'It can seldom if ever be in the interests of justice to re-sentence an offender for offences for which he was placed on probation after the commission of the crime for which he is subsequently sentenced, even if it is appropriate to revoke the probation order. Conviction of a further offence is a necessary but not a sufficient condition for re-sentencing under sch 2 para. 8'.

• In the case of a violent or sexual offence it may very occasionally be justified in re-sentencing the offender to impose a custodial sentence on grounds of protecting the public from serious harm. In *R v Powell* (1992) 13 Cr App R(S) 202, the offender had been convicted of indecent assault and was made subject of a probation order with a requirement of residence at a hostel specialising in the treatment of sexual offenders. He was initially prosecuted in breach proceedings for a failure to comply with the rules and subsequently absconded. Further breach proceedings were initiated and the order was revoked and he received a custodial sentence, subsequently upheld by the Court of Appeal which noted that his failure to respond to the order reinforced concern for the risk to the public. However, this case was decided in the context of the now repealed public protection provisions of CJA 1982. The public protection provisions of CJA 1991 have been interpreted more narrowly and it is possible that an offender presenting sufficient risk of serious harm will have little chance of a community sentence in the first instance.

• The offender should receive appropriate allowance for any period spent in custody prior to the imposition of the now revoked community sentence.

- Where a custodial sentence is imposed for the further offence and a consecutive custodial sentence is imposed for the original offence, the court should have regard to the 'totality principle' and adjust the sentence downwards if the impact of the combined sentences would be too severe for the overall seriousness of the offender's behaviour (*R v Anderson* (1982) 4 Cr App R(S) 252).

In addition to these considerations, the offender's degree of compliance with the order will also be significant and is now addressed separately.

Extent of Compliance

In dealing afresh with the offender, the court *shall* 'take into account the extent to which the offender has complied with the requirements of the relevant order' (sch 2 paras, 3(2)(a), 4(2)(a), 7(4) and 8(4)). In a number of cases prior to CJA 1991 the Court of Appeal indicated that credit should be given for partial compliance with community service orders, for example:

R v Paisley (1979) 1 Cr App R(S) 196, where credit was given for completion of 61 out of 100 hours despite breach of the order, so that the sentence of six months imprisonment imposed for the original offence was varied to allow the offender's immediate release.

R v Cook (1985) 7 Cr App R(S) 249, where credit was given for completion of 61 out of 80 hours, allowing the custodial sentence in place of the revoked CSO to be concurrent to the sentence imposed for a further offence rather than consecutive.

Though credit is 'a matter of fact and degree' in each case (according to the Court of Appeal in *Cook*), these decisions might suggest that credit will only be given where a substantial proportion of the order has been completed. However, in *R v Whittingham* (1986) 8 Cr App R(S) 116, credit was given where only 68 out of 180 hours had been performed. Credit for partial compliance with a probation order is clearly a less easy matter to quantify and to assess.

Hours of work undertaken *after* the initiation of breach proceedings can be taken into account in mitigation though the completion of the total number of hours at that stage is still only of mitigatory weight and does not free the offender from jeopardy (*R v Tebbutt* (1988) 10 Cr App R(S) 88 where the fact that the offender was prompted to complete his order only at that late stage clearly diminished the weight accorded).

Note that the phrasing of the requirement to take compliance into account goes beyond the giving of credit for satisfactory performance and appears to give scope to draw negative conclusions from an unsatisfactory record of compliance, albeit that this has not prompted the initiation of breach proceedings. In pre-CJA 1991 law it was clear that the court should not seek in re-sentencing the offender primarily to punish him or her for any defiance of the order (*R v Simpson* [1983] Crim LR 820) but in *breach* proceedings it is now permissible for the court to 'assume, in the case of an offender who has wilfully and persistently failed to comply with requirements that s/he has refused to give consent to a community sentence which has been proposed by the court and requires that consent' (paras. 3(2)(b) and 4(2)(b)). Such an assumption permits the court to impose a custodial sentence under CJA 1991 s1(3) for an offence which would not otherwise attract a custodial sentence. The issue of 'fault' in *revocation* proceedings is pursued further below.

Revocation Proceedings and Offender Default

As outlined on page 55, the Court of Appeal has indicated (*R v Jackson* (1984) 6 Cr App R(S) 202) that if the facts suggest a failure to comply, it is preferable for a prosecution for breach to be initiated rather than revocation proceedings, so that the facts can be placed on a proper evidential basis. In the earlier case of *R v Goscombe* (1981) 3 Cr App R(S) 61, the relevant officer applied for a community service order to be revoked after the offender had completed only 22 out of 120 hours in the first six months. The offender had experienced health problems but the court concluded that these were not the decisive factor and that he was also at fault. Though the *Jackson* principle that this should be tested in evidence rather than left to the court to conclude on its own reading of the history of the order seems entirely preferable, the *Goscombe* decision does suggest that the offender may be at greater risk of a custodial sentence in revocation proceedings if non-compliance has arisen, in part at least, through their own fault.

Compare *R v Fielding* [1993] Crim LR 229 where the offender was unable to continue his community service order because of a back injury. The Court of Appeal concluded that it was improper to impose a custodial sentence for the original offence because the offender's inability to comply was through no fault of his own. This decision leaves unclear what would be the court's view where the changed circumstances prompting the revocation application have arisen from a deliberate choice on the part of the offender, *eg* to take employment which is incompatible with CS commitments.

Imposing a Further Community Order

Revocation of a community order does not prevent the re-sentencing of the offender to a further community order, even an order of an identical nature to that now revoked: *R v Havant Justices ex parte Jacobs* [1957] 1 WLR 365, where a further probation order was held to be properly imposed following breach proceedings in place of a previous probation order. In each instance of re-sentencing following revocation, the offender's suitability for a further community order will need to be reconsidered afresh, albeit in the light of the experience of the previous unsuccessful order.

Coinciding Crown and Magistrates' Orders

Particular problems arise where an offender is subject both to a community order imposed by a magistrates' court and to a similar order imposed at Crown Court, as illustrated by *R v Meredith* [1994] Crim LR 142, outlined on page 6. After determining that the offender had failed to comply with CS requirements, the supervising court sought to remit the offender to the Crown Court in respect of both community service orders. The Crown Court revoked both orders and re-sentenced the offender, imposing custodial sentences for the original offences. Though the Court of Appeal upheld this exercise of jurisdiction, the statutory basis for this decision is hard to follow. There is no power under sch 2 paras. 3 or 7 for the supervising court to send an offender to the Crown Court to be dealt with in respect of a magistrates' court order, in either breach or revocation proceedings. Further, the Crown Court is not empowered under sch 2 paras. 4 or 8, when opting to revoke its own order, to assume jurisdiction over the magistrates' court order. A more cumbersome but more statutorily correct approach in *Meredith* would have required the Crown Court to resolve the future of the order made by that Court and then for the offender to have appeared before the lower court to resolve the outstanding order made by that court, in the light of the Crown Court's decision.

9.
AUTOMATIC CONDITIONAL RELEASE LICENCE

The following 'short-term prisoners' are subject to ACR licence on early release:

(a) prisoners aged 18 or over at the point of release serving terms of 12 months or more but less than four years;

(b) prisoners aged under 18 at the point of release serving terms of over 12 months but less than four years (*ie* those serving exactly 12 months are not subject to ACR provisions).

Licence Conditions

Prisoners and those serving sentences of detention in a young offender institution or detention under CYPA 1933 s53(2) who are eligible for automatic release on licence are normally released on 'standard' licence, paragraph 1 of which states:

'You will be under the supervision of a probation officer or a social worker of a local authority social services department and must comply with the conditions of this licence'.

After stating the commencement and expiry dates of supervision (para. 2), the licence instructs the offender to report on release without delay to a specified probation officer/social worker (para. 3) and thereafter 'you must place yourself under the supervision of whichever probation officer or social worker is nominated for this purpose from time to time' (para. 4). Para. 5 states the specific requirements of the supervision period:

While under supervision you must:

(i) keep in touch with your supervising officer in accordance with any reasonable instructions that you may from time to time be given;

(ii) if required, receive visits from your supervising officer at your home at reasonable hours and for reasonable periods;

(iii) live where reasonably approved by your supervising officer and notify him or her in advance of any proposed change of address;

(iv) undertake only such employment as your supervising officer reasonably approves and notify him or her in advance of any proposed change in employment or occupation;

(v) not travel outside the United Kingdom without obtaining the prior permission of your supervising officer;

(vi) not take any action which would jeopardise the objectives of your supervision, namely to protect the public, prevent you from re-offending and secure your successful reintegration into the community.

Note that the licence does not designate any petty sessional area and there is thus no 'supervising court' responsible for judicial oversight of the licence. Nor is responsibility lodged with a specific Probation Service or a designated local authority. The scheme is designed to be very flexible for supervision and enforcement purposes.

Additional Requirements

The Governor of the prison establishment from which the prisoner is released has a discretion to approve additional conditions in exceptional cases, on the recommendation or with the approval of the supervising officer 'in the interests of devising an effective programme of supervision'. Such conditions cannot be devised in an *ad hoc* way but must be selected from a list of approved conditions, as outlined in Chapter 11, where additional conditions are more likely to be inserted. A recommendation for additional licence conditions must be based on clearly identifiable reasons.

Variation of Requirements

There is no power for a court to vary ACR licence conditions. The only scope for variation, addition or deletion of a condition is for the supervising officer to apply to the Governor of the releasing prison, outlining the reasons for the request and forwarding a copy of the original licence. If the request is approved, a fresh licence will be issued and sent to the supervising officer who must serve it upon the offender and then send three copies, signed by the prisoner, back to the establishment for retention and distribution. If the prisoner refuses to sign or accept the fresh licence the supervisor should certify the licence to the effect that the variation has been explained but not signed for or accepted. If the offender changes address to another area (with the agreement of the supervising officer) and a change of supervising officer is necessary, this is achieved by administrative transfer of responsibility and negotiation between teams and areas (see *National Standard for Supervision Before and After Release from Custody*, 1994 paras. 45–46). The only crucial consideration in this instance is that the offender is informed clearly of the change in nominated supervisor, so that the offender knows whose instructions and visits to receive, to whom proposed changes of address or employment should be notified and whose permission is required for travel abroad. If a prisoner is returned to custody on suspension of licence by a court and re-released before the licence expiry date, additional conditions may then be included in the licence freshly issued at that point.

Expiry

An ACR licence remains in force until the date on which the prisoner would (but for their release) have served three-quarters of their sentence (CJA 1991 s37(1)) but this is qualified by the provision in CJA 1991 s41(3)(a) that time spent on remand shall not have the effect of reducing the period of licence to less than one-quarter of sentence, even if this extends the licence period beyond the three-quarters point. However, the licence cannot run beyond the full term (100% point) of sentence, where this intervenes within that normal minimum period.

Refusal to Give a Release Address

The scheme is posited on the basis that the prisoner will co-operate in the first instance by disclosing a release address so that initial reporting instructions can be given and a supervising officer nominated. As there is no mechanism to delay release in the event of non-co-operation, the system has limited sanctions if the prisoner refuses to give a release address, as Circular Instruction 27/1992 paras. 25–6 recognises:

> 'If the home area is not known, it may be necessary to instruct the prisoner to report to the duty officer at a probation office in the petty sessional area where the prisoner

was tried for the current offence. If agreed with the Probation Service, and as a last resort, part or all of the discharge grant may be sent to the reporting office as an incentive to turn up'.

The aim is clearly to assign supervisory responsibility in all instances and to make this clear to the prisoner so that the onus rests with the offender to make contact with that supervisor who will be responsible for initiating prosecution in the event of default. The most difficulty may arise with the genuinely homeless prisoner who claims to have no fixed pre-determined plans for their initial release period and is reluctant to make any advance commitment to go to any specific destination. The system cannot hope to be totally watertight but in the last resort responsibility can be assigned to an officer serving the magistrates' court in which the prosecution leading to the custodial sentence was initiated.

Failure to Comply

The supervisor will initially refer to the *National Standard for Supervision Before and After Release from Custody* (1994) which makes the following points.

• Breach action may be taken at any stage in the licence and after only one failure to comply, if the assessment of risk or the seriousness of the alleged breach justifies this (para. 52).

• Upon failure to report in accordance with the initial reporting instruction, the supervisor should (a) check with the prison establishment that release took place, (b) if the prisoner was released, visit the offender's address within one working day, (c) where necessary arrange for the prison and police to be informed immediatley (para. 51).

• Upon any failure to comply with a licence condition the supervising officer should either:

    –   institute breach action immediately; or

    –   issue a formal written warning of the likely consequences of further failure to comply, to be given in person to the offender, who should be asked to sign to confirm that s/he has understood its contents, and a copy served on the offender. Where the offender refuses to sign, this should be recorded (para. 53).

• 'If the offender fails to attend or to comply on a second occasion, breach action should be instituted or a further and final warning should be given following the same procedure as for the first' (para. 54).

• 'If the offender fails to attend or to comply on a third occasion, breach action should be instituted, even if this occurs towards the end of the licence' (para. 55).

Prosecuting Breach

CJA 1991 s38

(1) A short-term prisoner:

    (a)   who is released on licence under this Part; and

(b) who fails to comply with such conditions as may for the time being be specified in the licence,

shall be liable on summary conviction to a fine not exceeding level 3 (currently £1,000) on the standard scale.

(2) The magistrates' court by which a person is convicted of an offence under subsection (1) above may, whether or not it passes any other sentence on him:

(a) suspend the licence for a period not exceeding six months; and

(b) order him to be recalled to prison for the period during which the licence is so suspended.

(3) On the suspension of the licence of any person under this section, he shall be liable to be detained in pursuance of his sentence and, if at large, shall be deemed to be unlawfully at large.

Failure to comply with an ACR licence condition is thus a non-imprisonable summary offence. Though the court has power to order recall to custody, this is not the imposition of a fresh sentence, merely the resumption of the custodial phase of the existing sentence.

Application of PACE

Because a breach of ACR is a criminal offence, the investigating probation officer should adhere to the provisions of PACE 1984 (see *National Standard*, 1994 para. 57), in particular:

Cautioning 'A person whom there are grounds to suspect of an offence must be cautioned before any questions about it (or further questions if it is his or her answers to previous questions that provide grounds for suspicion) are put to him or her for the purpose of obtaining evidence which may be given to a court on prosecution' (Code C para. 10.1). The wording of the caution will change after implementation of CJPOA 1994 and the consequent variation of the 'right to silence'. The controversial proposed wording of the new style caution states:

'You do not have to say anything. But if you do not mention something which you later use in your defence, the court may decide that your failure to mention it now strengthens the case against you. A record will be made of anything you say and it may be given in evidence if you are brought to trial'.

The person being questioned should be told that they are free to leave if they choose to do so.

When there is a break in questioning under caution, the interviewing officer must ensure that the person being questioned is aware that s/he remains under caution (para. 10.5). If the interviewed person is a juvenile or mentally disordered, an 'appropriate adult' should be present and the caution repeated in that person's presence.

Legal Advice The suspected offender should be reminded of his/her entitlement to legal advice prior to the commencement or re-commencement of any interview. This reminder should be noted in the record of interview (Code C para. 11.2).

Recording An accurate record must be made of each interview with the suspected offender, stating the place and timing of the interview and who was present. This should be made during the course of the interview or as soon as practicable after its completion and should constitute either a verbatim record of what has been said or an account of the interview which adequately and accurately summarises it (Code C para. 11.5).

Initiating Prosecution

Prosecution is initiated in the usual way by the laying of an information, an example of which is included in this chapter. As there is no specified supervising court, jurisdiction to try the case is determined by MCA 1980 s2 which gives a magistrates' court power to try any summary offence which allegedly occurred within the county (or London commission area) for which the court acts (s 2(1)). Subject to limited exceptions, a magistrates' court may not try a summary offence occurring outside its county.

This restriction will not usually cause difficulty. If an offender has failed to keep an appointment with their supervisor, prosecution will naturally proceed in the court with jurisdiction for the area in which the supervisor's work is situated (the local court). However, it may appear more problematic to initiate a s38 prosecution in the local court if the allegation is that the offender has undertaken something which s/he was not entitled to do without permission, *eg* travelling outside the UK without prior permission. It might appear that the offence has occurred elsewhere, even abroad. These pitfalls can be avoided by appropriate drafting of the information, effectively translating a licence condition default into an offence by casting the allegation in terms of the offender's *failure* to fulfil a requirement, in this instance the obtaining of prior permission. That failure will have occurred within the jurisdiction of the local court.

The exception to the 'county' rule of s2(1) which may be helpful for enforcement purposes allows a magistrates' court to deal with any summary offence, whether committed in or outside the county, where an accused person is already being tried for another offence before that court (s 2(6)). This means that if an ACR prisoner is being prosecuted for a fresh offence in another part of the country, the supervisor may find it more convenient to initiate a s38 prosecution in that distant court (with the assistance of colleagues in that area) so that both matters can be dealt with together rather than in two separate proceedings. However, obvious practical problems could arise if the s38 allegation is contested and it is necessary to bring evidence at trial.

Summons or Warrant?

Though it would normally be appropriate to seek a summons to bring the offender before the court, this may be considered less effective than a warrant not backed for bail to secure the arrest of an offender (for example, one who has failed to report on release or has subsequently changed address without advance notification) when their current whereabouts are unknown. A warrant can certainly be issued in respect of a non-imprisonable offence where the accused's address is insufficiently established for a summons to be served (MCA 1980 s1(4)).

However, there may nevertheless be merit in proceeding by summons, to be served by post to their last known place of abode, to take advantage of the provision in MCA 1980 s11(1) allowing summary trial to take place in the absence of the defendant. If a warrant without bail is issued there may be a considerable delay before the defendant is arrested and brought to court, by which time their licence may well have expired. The consequence of expiry is that an offender can no longer be recalled to prison, thus leaving the court with power only to fine the offender. As s/he would by then be no longer subject to supervision requirements, the fine would not serve to re-engage the offender in any constructive work but would merely serve as a somewhat limited demonstration of the authority of the licence.

Trial in Absence of Defendant

To proceed with trial when the defendant fails to appear, it must be proved to the satisfaction of the court that 'the summons was served on the accused within what appears to the court to be a reasonable time before the trial... or that the accused has appeared on a previous occasion to answer to the information' (s 11(2)).

Upon conviction in the offender's absence, the court may exercise its discretion to suspend the licence and order recall under s38(2). The offender is then unlawfully 'at large' and remains liable to be arrested and returned to prison for the period so ordered, even if the date on which the licence would otherwise have expired is passed in the interim.

Strict Liability?

Unlike other statutory provisions governing breach (including CJA 1991 s65(6) regarding supervision on release from YOI), s38(1) does not refer to failure to comply 'without reasonable excuse'. This would appear on a literal reading to imply an offence of 'strict liability', *ie* one for which the offender can be convicted simply on the bald fact of non-compliance irrespective of any excuse or justification. However, it is a principle of law that in cases where Parliament has not made it clear that strict liability is intended, the courts will interpret the legislation with a presumption that Parliament did not intend to punish a blameless individual and will read an element of blameworthiness into the statute. In any event, the relevant *National Standard* (para. 50) anticipates the offender may have an acceptable explanation for their non-compliance and that an incident should be regarded as a failure to comply only where the explanation is not considered acceptable.

After Conviction

If the offender pleads or is found guilty, the court's powers are limited to imposing a fine or suspending the licence, or both. However, if the licence has expired, by the date of conviction or sentence, the offender cannot be recalled to prison as the recall period can run only from the date the breach was proved in court, not from the date that the breach was committed or the information was laid. It can thus be to the offender's advantage to delay the process for as long as possible, *eg* by entering a tactical not guilty plea.

There is no requirement for the court to receive a pre-sentence report prior to sentence but if the offender is eligible for suspension of licence and recall then the court is almost certain to seek advice from the supervisor or the Probation Service. Such advice is far less pertinent if the court merely has power of fine. The relevant *National Standard* advises that a report should be given orally or in writing, as requested by the court, addressing the following points (para. 58):

BANKINGWELL MAGISTRATES COURT

Date :	8 October 1994
To (accused) :	Owen Gary WELLS **DoB :** 25.12.1950
Address :	Currently unknown. Last known address: Flat 5, 28 Robert Maxwell Avenue, Bankingwell, Boomshire

Details of Order

Early Release Licence for short term prisoners

Court which imposed sentence of custody :	Crown Court at Costingham
Date of sentence :	**Duration of sentence :** 30 months
Offence in respect of which sentence imposed :	Obtaining a pecuniary advantage by deception
Date of release : 15 June 1994	**Date licence expires :** 31 January 1995

Information laid by :	Seema PATEL, Probation Officer
Address :	Probation Office, Nelson Mandela House, 94 Cheapside, Bankingwell.

Who (upon oath) states that the accused has failed to comply with the requirements of Early Release Licence

Alleged failure to comply with condition(s) :
Failed to notify his supervising officer of his proposed change of address, leaving his last known address between 20 September and 2 October without notice or authorisation (Criminal Justice Act 1991 s38(1)).

Taken (and sworn) before me

Justices' Clerk/
Justice of the Peace

Return date information :	
Court date and time :	
Delete as applicable : ~~Summons *~~ ~~Warrant with bail *~~ Warrant no bail *	

Information for Breach of conditions of Early Release Licence

- the offender's response to supervision before and after instigation of breach action;

- an explanation for the breach;

- an assessment of risk;

- a recommendation about how reasonable it would be for the offender to continue under supervision, be fined or returned to prison, given an absolute/conditional discharge or dealt with under the range of other sentencing options applicable to non-imprisonable summary offences.

Recall to Custody

There is no provision allowing for the recall of an ACR offender by the Home Office if they are acting in a way which gives serious cause for concern. The only basis for enforcement is by prosecution for breach. As breach is a non-imprisonable offence there is only very limited scope for an offender to be *remanded* in custody following an allegation of breach of licence. Sch 1 Part II of the Bail Act 1976 specifies certain very limited exceptions to the right to bail of defendants accused or convicted of non-imprisonable offences. Thus a defendant need not be granted bail if s/he:

(i) has absconded on a previous occasion after being granted bail in criminal proceedings and, in view of that, the court believes he or she would fail to surrender to custody if granted bail on the present occasion; or

(ii) should be kept in custody for their own protection (or welfare, if a juvenile).

As Circular Instruction 27/1992 points out (para. 43): 'a person accused of a very serious breach may also have committed a criminal offence and may, by their failure to comply with supervision, give cause for concern that they would not surrender if released on bail' in respect of that fresh offence.

Impact of Suspension upon Licence

If licence is suspended, the offender's overall length of licence is not affected and their licence period is not extended by the period of time spent back in custody. If the prisoner is re-released before the licence expiry date, supervision requirements resume for the outstanding period and the prisoner is issued with a new licence containing fresh reporting instructions. The new licence may contain additional conditions which were not part of the original licence.

10.
SUPERVISION ON RELEASE FROM YOI DETENTION

Liability to statutory supervision under CJA 1991 s65 arises in three instances:

(a) where a young offender aged under 18 (at the point of early release) is serving a YOI term of 12 months or less;

(b) where a young offender aged 18 to under 22 (at the point of early release) is serving a YOI term of under 12 months;

(c) where a young offender is released on ACR licence but their licence period is for less than three months and s/he has not reached their 22nd birthday at the time of licence expiry.

The provisions for the enforcement of YOI supervision are very similar to those pertaining to ACR licence but there are a number of differences which make it convenient to set out procedure in this separate outline, which nevertheless cross-references extensively to the ACR chapter. The same *National Standard* governs both forms of supervision.

Notice of Supervision

Eligible young offenders are released not on licence but on 'notice of supervision' (s65(5)). The requirement terms of notice of supervision are identical to the conditions contained in a standard ACR licence (see page 85) but there is no discretion to add further conditions from the list of approved extra conditions, either at the time of release or subsequently. The notice does not specify a petty sessions area for the purposes of judicial oversight of the supervision period or a particular Probation Service or local authority area. The arrangements for initial reporting, including the problems relating to non-co-operative or homeless trainees, and for transfer upon the offender's subsequent change of address, are the same as in the case of ACR licence.

Duration

The period of supervision lasts for three months from date of release except in the case of offenders under (c) above who transfer status from ACR licencee to s65 supervisee for a period terminating three months after their date of release. In all instances supervision terminates automatically on the offender's 22nd birthday if this occurs within three months of their date of release.

Failure to Comply

The scope within the *National Standard* for dealing with failures to comply by means other than prosecution such as formal warnings are as set out in the ACR chapter.

Prosecution for Breach of Requirements

CJA 1991 s65

(6) A person who without reasonable excuse fails to comply with a requirement imposed under subsection (5) above shall be liable on summary conviction:

(a) to a fine not exceeding level 3 on the standard scale (currently £1,000); or

(b) to an appropriate custodial sentence for a period not exceeding 30 days, but not liable to be dealt with in any other way.

(7) In subsection (6) above 'appropriate custodial sentence' means:

(a) a sentence of imprisonment, if the offender has attained the age of 21 years when he is sentenced; and

(b) a sentence of detention in a young offender institution, if he has not attained that age.

Breach of a s65 requirement is thus a summary but imprisonable offence (Circular Instruction 27/1992 claims that breach is not a criminal offence but this is erroneous; CJA 1982 s1A(4), which permits a breach to be punished by a period of YOI less than the normal minimum term, specifically recognises a breach as an offence). The requirements of PACE apply (see page 88). Prosecution is initiated in the usual way by laying an information, an example of which is included in this chapter. See the ACR chapter with regard to questions of a court's jurisdiction to try a summary offence under MCA 1980 s2. Because the offence is imprisonable, a justice before whom an information is laid on oath and in writing has power under MCA 1980 s1(1)(b) to issue a warrant for the offender's arrest, instead of issuing a summons. The provisions of s65(6) do not require the information to be laid during the continuance of the supervision period, merely that the failure occurred during that period. Commencement of prosecution is thus subject to the general provision of MCA 1980 s127(1) concerning the time within which summary trial should take place and the court's discretion regarding delay of process (see page 5).

As the offence may be punished by a fresh custodial sentence rather than by recall to custody, the power is not in any way tied to the time scale of the original custodial term or to the expiry of the supervision period. Consequently, the urgency which may apply in ACR licence enforcement to bring the matter before the court during the licence period and to proceed, if necessary, in the absence of the offender does not apply here. If trial did proceed in the offender's absence, there would be no power to impose a custodial sentence (MCA 1980 s11(3)). Conversely, there is no provision within s65 for the offender to be 'unlawfully at large' and liable to be detained in pursuance of sentence. However, as a warrant not backed for bail can be issued, whether instead of proceeding by summons (under MCA 1980 s1(1)(b)) or on the offender's non-appearance in answer to summons (under MCA 1980 s13(1)), the offender can be subject to powers of arrest and to be detained in custody to be brought before the court.

Following Conviction

Although there is limited power of sentence and no scope for the court to deal with the matter by imposing a community sentence, the court is likely to expect or request a report from the supervisor or the Probation Service. This is not necessarily a pre-sentence report within the provisions of CJA 1991 s3(5), and can be given orally or in writing, but should address the points suggested in the *National Standard for Supervision Before and After Release from Custody* (para. 76), as detailed on page 92.

If a custodial sentence is imposed, the provisions of s65(8) apply and the offender is not liable to an additional period of supervision. Any residential period of supervision arising from the original notice remains to be served.

CJA 1991 s65

(8) A person released from a custodial sentence passed under subsection (6) above shall not be liable to a period of supervision in consequence of his conviction under that subsection, but his conviction shall not prejudice any liability to supervision to which he was previously subject, and that liability shall accordingly continue until the end of the supervision period.

ARDLEIGH CRICKETT MAGISTRATES COURT

Date :	1 October 1994
To (accused) :	Keenan ABEL **DoB :** 29.2.1977
Address :	11 Stumps Lane, Ardleigh Crickett, Loamshire

Details of Order

Young Offender Institution Supervision

Court which imposed sentence of custody to YOI:	Ardleigh Crickett Youth Court
Date of sentence : 8.6.1994	**Duration of sentence :** 4 months
Offence in respect of which sentence imposed :	Burglary
Date of release from Institution: 8 August 1994	**Date supervision expires :** 7 November 1995

Information laid by :	William G.GRACE, Probation Officer
Address :	Probation Office, The Law Courts, Pavilion Road, Ardleigh Crickett, Loamshire.

Who (upon oath) states that the accused has failed to comply with the requirements of Young Offender Institution Supervision

Alleged failure to comply with requirement(s) :
Having been instructed on 10 September 1994 to attend for interview with the supervising officer on 18 September 1994, failed to do so (Criminal Justice Act 1991 s65(6)).

Taken (and sworn) before me

Justices' Clerk/
Justice of the Peace

Return date information :	Ardleigh Crickett Youth Court
Court date and time :	on 22 October 1994 at 9.30 am
Delete as applicable :	**Summons** ~~Warrant with bail~~ ~~Warrant no bail~~

Information for Breach of requirements of Young Offender Institution Supervision

11.
DISCRETIONARY CONDITIONAL RELEASE

All 'long-term' prisoners, including those subject to YOI and CYPA 1933 s53 detention for terms of four years or more, fall in the category of 'discretionary release' whether released on parole at the Home Secretary's discretion after serving one-half of sentence or automatically after serving two-thirds of sentence. Enforcement in this context is not subject to judicial oversight but is a matter of executive discretion, conducted by the Home Office through the Parole Unit, in consultation with or on the recommendation of the Parole Board.

Licence Conditions

The standard conditions are as specified for short-term prisoners on ACR licence, detailed on page 85. Additional conditions may be inserted, chosen from the following list of approved extra conditions, on the recommendation of or in consultation with the officer who will supervise the licence:

1. Attending upon a duly qualified psychiatrist/psychologist/medical practitioner for such care, supervision or treatment as that practitioner recommends.

2. Not to engage in any work or other organised activity involving a person under a specified age.

3. To reside at a specified address and not to leave without prior approval of supervising officer; thereafter to reside as directed by supervising officer.

4. Not to reside in the same household as any child under a specified age.

5. Not to seek to approach or communicate with wife/former wife/child(ren)/grandchildren/other named persons without prior approval of supervising officer and named social services department.

6. Comply with any requirements reasonably imposed by supervising officer for purpose of ensuring that licensee address alcohol/drug/sexual/gambling/solvent abuse/debt/offending behaviour problems at specified course or centre (where appropriate).

Variation of Licence

Additional conditions may be inserted, varied or cancelled during the course of the licence period. The supervising officer must apply to the Parole Unit, giving a full account of the reasons for the request, and, if the request is agreed by the Parole Board, the changes are referred to the Governor of the establishment from which the prisoner was released so that a fresh licence can be issued. The supervisor should then serve the licence, explaining to the offender the changes and the reasons for these and requesting the offender to sign the licence. If the offender refuses, the supervisor should certify the licence to the effect that the alterations have been explained but that the offender was unwilling to sign or accept it.

Nominated Supervisor

The supervising officer is normally a probation officer but, for a young offender released under the age of 22, may be a social worker of a local authority social services department

(CJA 1991 s43(5)). If the licence is for a substantial period, responsibility for supervision can be transferred from Social Services to the Probation Service, by inter-agency agreement, notified to the Parole Unit and to the Chief Constable for the offender's home area. Similarly, if an offender is moving permanently to another area (with the agreement of the supervising officer) transfer of supervisory responsibility can be achieved by administrative negotiation, with notification of the new address and supervisor to the Parole Unit and to the Chief Constable for the offender's present home area. In both instances it is essential for the offender to be notified of the change so that s/he is clear from whom instructions should be received and who should be notified of and approve proposed changes of address, employment, etc.

Failure to Comply and Cause for Concern

Breach action will normally arise from failure to comply with licence conditions. However, as Circular Instruction 26/1992 (para. 17) points out:

> 'Unlike short-term prisoners whose recall will be dealt with by magistrates' courts, there is no requirement to prove a specific breach and recall may be pre-emptive'.

This is amplified by the *National Standard for Supervision Before and After Release from Custody* (1994) which identifies as factors to be taken into consideration the following (para. 59):

- situations where the offender's behaviour is such that further serious offences are likely to be committed;

- grounds for believing that the safety of the public may for any reason be at risk;

- the possibility of the offender's behaviour bringing the licence system into disrepute; or impeding supervision activity.

Among specific issues addressed by the *National Standard*:

Failure to Report on Release The Parole Board should be informed via the Parole Unit with a recommendation from a Chief Officer grade (or local authority equivalent) as to further action (para. 51).

Supervising Officer's Concern 'The Parole Board should be informed if the supervising officer has concerns, whether or not recall is being recommended at this stage' (para. 52).

Failure to Attend an Appointment or other Failure to Comply Immediate breach action should be instituted or a formal written warning should be issued indicating the likely consequences of further failure to comply. A warning should be given in person to the offender who should sign to confirm that he or she has understood its contents. Where the offender refuses to sign, this should be recorded (para. 53). On failure to attend or to comply on a second occasion breach action should be instituted or a further and final warning should be given, as above. On a third occasion, of failure to comply, breach action should be initiated (paras. 54–55).

Instigating Recall When the supervisor's manager determines that recall proceedings should be instigated, a Chief Officer grade (or local authority equivalent) should submit a written report, with a recommendation to the Parole Board via the Parole Unit. 'The report should contain as much relevant background information as possible, say whether recall is considered to be necessary and indicate whether the offender has previously received written warnings from the (supervisory agency)' (para. 59). The

Parole Board will then decide whether the offender's behaviour is sufficiently serious to justify suspension of licence and recall or prison or whether to issue a formal warning.

Revocation of Licence

CJA 1991 s39

(1) If recommended to do so by the Board in the case of a long-term or life prisoner who has been released on licence under this Part, the Secretary of State may revoke his licence and recall him to prison.

(2) The Secretary of State may revoke the licence of any such person and recall him to prison without a recommendation by the Board, where it appears to him that it is expedient in the public interest to recall that person before such a recommendation is practicable.

(6) On the revocation of the licence of any person under this section, he shall be liable to be detained in pursuance of his sentence and, if at large, shall be deemed to be unlawfully at large.

'Emergency' recall under s39(2) may be justified where the risk to the safety of the public appears so great as to justify immediate action to recall the offender to prison. Where the supervisor's manager determines that there is a case for emergency recall, a request for the offender's licence to be revoked should be made through a Chief Officer grade to the Parole Unit by telephone, contacting the duty officer if the call is outside office hours, followed by the submission of a written report, preferably faxed to the Unit, detailing why rapid recall is considered essential.

Rights and Procedure Following Recall

CJA 1991 s39

(3) A person recalled to prison under subsection (1) or (2) above:

(a) may make representations in writing with respect to his recall; and

(b) on his return to prison, shall be informed of the reasons for his recall and of his right to make representations.

(4) The Secretary of State shall refer to the Board:

(a) the case of a person recalled under subsection (1) above who makes representations under subsection (3) above; and

(b) the case of a person recalled under subsection (2) above.

Where the Board subsequently recommends the immediate release of a recalled long-term prisoner, the Home Secretary shall put this into effect (s 39(5)).

If not released on the recommendation or direction of the Parole Board, a long-term detainee who has been recalled by the Board under s39(1) shall be released unconditionally at the three-quarters point of sentence, *ie* the point at which the licence would have expired (s 33(3)(b)). CJA 1991 is silent as to the fate of the long-term detainee recalled directly by the Home Secretary under the 'emergency' power of s39(2), though it would seem anomalous that these prisoners should (by implication) remain in custody until completion of the full term of their sentence. This appears to be a statutory oversight rather than an intended consequence.

12.
SECURE TRAINING ORDERS

To be introduced by the Criminal Justice and Public Order Act 1994 (at time of writing still progressing towards Royal Assent), the secure training order is a custodial sentence for 12–14 year olds combining in equal proportions a period of detention in a secure training centre with a follow up period of supervision. As the enabling legislation still awaits its final form, only a tentative and rudimentary outline of supervision enforcement follows.

Supervision

The offender shall be under the supervision of a probation officer assigned to the PSA in which the offender resides, a social worker of the social services department for the local authority area in which the offender resides, or such other person as the Home Secretary may designate (CJPOA 1994 s3(2)-(5)).

Notice of Supervision

The offender will receive a notice of supervision prior to the commencement of supervision specifying the category of person for the time being responsible for their supervision and 'any requirements with which s/he must for the time being comply' (s3(6)(a) and (b)). At this stage it is not known what standard requirements will be included in the notice of supervision or whether additional requirements may be optionally included. Scope for variation of requirements will presumably be on the same basis as for ACR licence.

Length of Supervision Period

The length of supervision will be linked to the total length of the order determined by the court, being one half of that total period. As the minimum and maximum terms of the order are six months to two years, supervision will be for a period between three and 12 months.

Jurisdiction

Jurisdiction for enforcement purposes can be exercised by a youth court acting for 'a relevant PSA', defined by s4(2) as one of the following:

(a)   the PSA in which the secure training centre is situated;

(b)   if the order was imposed by a youth court, the PSA for the youth court which made the order; or

(c)   the PSA in which the offender for the time being resides.

Jurisdiction is thus not the exclusive province of one court, though (c) is the most likely venue in enforcement proceedings. No PSA is specified in the order and so if the offender moves address to a new area, jurisdiction under (c) correspondingly transfers with them without the need for any application for variation.

Failure to Comply

CJPOA 1994 s4

(1) Where a secure training order has been made as respects an offender and it appears on information to a justice of the peace acting for a relevant petty sessions area that the offender has failed to comply with requirements under section 3(6)(b) the justice may issue a summons requiring the offender to appear at the place and time specified in the summons before a youth court acting for the area or, if the information is in writing and on oath, may issue a warrant for the offender's arrest requiring him or her to be brought before such a court.

(3) If it is proved to the satisfaction of the youth court before which an offender appears or is brought under this section that s/he has failed to comply with requirements under section 3(6)(b) that court may:

(a) order the offender to be detained in a secure training centre for such period, not exceeding the shorter of three months or the remainder of the period of the secure training order, as the court may specify, or

(b) impose on the offender a fine not exceeding level 3 on the standard scale.

These provisions have a hybrid appearance, specifying that a prosecution will be initiated in the manner prescribed by CJA 1991 sch 2 for breach of a community order, while a breach is punishable in a manner akin to a failure to comply with an ACR licence. Note that s4(1) does not require the order still to be 'in force' when the information is laid but the power of the court under s4(3)(a) to order that the offender is returned to a secure training centre is only available while the order remains in force. As with breach of an ACR licence, 'failure to comply' is not qualified by the words 'without reasonable excuse' but it appears proper to regard this as implicit. If the offender is returned to a secure training centre (for a period not exceeding three months) supervision requirements will resume if the order has not meanwhile expired, but their supervision period is not extended by the period of time spent back in custody nor does the further period at a secure training centre incur a fresh period of supervision of identical length.

13.
SUSPENDED SENTENCE SUPERVISION ORDERS

The suspended sentence supervision order (SSSO) is something of an endangered species. It may only be imposed by the Crown Court (when imposing a suspended sentence of more than six months for a single offence) and, having fluctuated in numbers between 2,000 and 2,500 imposed per year in the period 1985 to 1991, fell to 1,727 commencing in 1992, partly reflecting the changes affecting suspension of sentence introduced by CJA 1991 which provides that sentence may only be suspended in 'exceptional circumstances' (PCCA 1973 s22(2)). This order will thus become increasingly rare unless the 'exceptional circumstances' provision is interpreted rather more permissively.

Requirements

PCCA 1973 s26

(4) An offender in respect of whom a supervision order is in force shall keep in touch with the supervising officer in accordance with such instructions as he may from time to time be given by that officer and shall notify him of any change of address.

There is no provision for a SSSO to include any additional requirements.

Jurisdiction

The supervision order must specify the petty sessions area in which the offender resides or will reside (PCCA 1973 s26(3)). Oversight of the order thus lies with a magistrates' court acting for the specified PSA. The only exception is in respect of the discharge of a SSSO where the Crown Court has specifically reserved that power to itself (see below).

The length of the supervision period is specified in the order and may be for the length of the operational period of the suspended sentence or for such shorter period as the court decides but may not exceed the operational period.

National Standards

There is no specific *National Standard* for SSSOs but 'as far as appropriate, supervision of offenders under a SSSO should be conducted in accordance with (the *National Standard* for probation orders)' (*National Standard*, 1994, para. 3).

Amendment

The only amendment which may be made to a SSSO is simply to substitute a new PSA for that specified in the order, where the offender moves to reside within another area. If a magistrates' court acting for the specified PSA is satisfied that the offender has changed or proposes to change address to another PSA, it may 'and on the application of the supervising officer shall amend the order' to specify the new PSA (s 26(6)). Judicial oversight thus transfers to a magistrates' court acting for the new area.

Application should be made in the same way as for the amendment of a probation order on change of residence (outlined on page 28), using a modified version of the appropriate form. It is not required to lay an information and the offender is not required to attend at court. When the Crown Court deals with an offender who is subject to a suspended sentence and opts not to bring the suspended term into effect, it may either make a supervision order where no order previously existed or may make a new order in place of any existing order (s 26(10)). Thus if the Court decides to extend the operational period of the suspended sentence, it could also extend the supervision period.

Breach of Requirements

Breach proceedings are initiated in the normal way by laying an information alleging a failure to comply. A summons or arrest warrant may then be issued to bring the offender before the court (PCCA 1973 s27(1) and (2)). Where it is established that the offender has failed 'without reasonable cause' to comply with any requirement, the court may impose a fine of up to £1,000, without prejudice to the continuance of the order (s 27(3)). Breach of a requirement is not a ground for activating the suspended term and the magistrates' court has no power to remit the offender back to the Crown Court.

Termination

An SSSO can be terminated prior to expiry by one of three ways:

(a)   where the Crown Court activates the suspended term;

(b)   where the Crown Court reviews the suspended sentence and opts to impose a new supervision order in place of the existing order under s26(1) (see above);

(c)   where the order is discharged under s26(9).

PCCA 1973 s26

(9) A supervision order may be discharged on the application of the supervising officer or the offender:

(a) if it was made by the Crown Court and included a direction reserving the power of discharging it to that court, by the Crown Court;

(b) in any other case by a magistrates' court acting for the petty sessions area for the time being specified in the order.

The provisions of s26(9) do not make clear the procedure to be adopted in discharge proceedings. If the application is made by the supervising officer, there is no provision to summon the offender before the court. The court should proceed to consider the application on the basis of the supervising officer's representations and report. If the court is unhappy with the merits of the application it has the option to decline it. If the application is made by the offender, the question arises whether the application can be made simply in writing or requires personal appearance. It seems open to the court's discretion how to proceed but the court will almost certainly require a report from the supervising officer before reaching a decision. Where the Crown Court has reserved power of discharge to itself, application should be made directly to that Court (consult the Crown Court liaison officer) and not via the supervising court.

14.
MONEY PAYMENT SUPERVISION ORDERS

The number of persons commencing a money payment supervision order (MPSO) supervised by the Probation Service has fallen from 6,460 in 1989 to 4,528 in 1992. This fall may reflect greater use of the scope to appoint an individual outside the Service (such as a member of the justices' clerk's department) to undertake supervision. The order is regulated by MCA 1980 s88 and is clearly intended to promote payment of financial penalties rather than to be a penalty in its own right or to restrict the liberty of the offender. It provides a measure of protection to the offender, particularly persons under 21, when committal to prison in default is being considered. It has been suggested that the MPSO may provide a means of offering some degree of formal assistance to low tariff offenders whose offences are insufficiently serious to merit a community order.

Duration

A MPSO is not imposed for a fixed term and remains in force while the person under supervision remains liable to pay the sum or until the order is either discharged or ceases to have effect (s 88(2)).

Supervisor's Responsibility

The responsibility is essentially twofold: to assist the offender and to give information to the court.

MCR 1981 r56

(2) It shall be the duty of any person for the time being appointed under MCA 1980 s88 to advise and befriend the offender with a view to inducing him to pay the sum adjudged to be paid and thereby avoid committal to custody and to give any information required by a magistrates' court about the offender's conduct and means.

The court in turn is under a duty to consult the supervisor before committing a supervised person to custody.

MCA 1980 s88

(6) Where an order placing a person under supervision with respect to a sum is in force, a magistrates' court shall not commit him to prison in default of payment of the sum, or for want of sufficient distress to satisfy the sum, unless the court has before committing him taken such steps as may be reasonably practicable to obtain from the person appointed for his supervision an oral or written report on the offender's conduct and means and has considered any report so obtained, in addition, in a case where an inquiry is required by section 82 above, to that inquiry.

Termination

A MPSO terminates upon:

(a)   payment of sum outstanding;

(b)   discharge of the order by the court that made it (s 88(3) which does not specify any procedure for seeking discharge. The supervisor should write to the justices' clerk requesting that their application for discharge should be listed for a suitable hearing opportunity before a fines enforcement court and prepare a short report in support of the application to be considered by the court);

(c)   the making of a transfer of fines order under MCA 1980 s89 where the offender is residing in another petty sessions area and enforcement of the liability is transferred to the new area. A MPSO cannot follow an offender to their new area and there is thus no scope for amending the order on change of residence;

(d)   the offender's committal to custody in default (though not upon the making of a suspended committal order).

MCA 1980 s88

(2) An order placing a person under supervision in respect of any sum shall remain in force so long as he remains liable to pay the sum or any part of it unless the order ceases to have effect or is discharged under subsection (3) below.

(3) An order under this section shall cease to have effect on the making of a transfer of fine order under section 89 below with respect to the sum adjudged to be paid and may be discharged by the court that made it, without prejudice in either case to the making of a new order.

15.
VARYING OR RESCINDING SENTENCE

Both the Crown Court and a magistrates' court have power to vary or rescind its decision as to sentence or other order, under the Supreme Court Act 1981 s47(2) and MCA 1980 s142(1) respectively. The power must be exercised within 28 days, that period commencing on the day on which the sentence or order was imposed or made.

Extent of the Power

The scope of this power is wide and may be used in the following instances, by no means confined to correcting minor errors in sentencing:

• To replace an invalid sentence or one which the court had no power to pass with a lawful sentence, *eg* where a young person aged 15 at the time of conviction is mistakenly sentenced to a community service or probation order, as may happen if sentence is passed after their 16th birthday.

• To replace a sentence which the court had power to pass but which was crucially flawed in some procedural way. The obvious possibility of this for the purposes of community sentence management would be a sentence requiring the offender's consent (probation, community service, combination and curfew orders, and certain requirements in supervision orders) where it becomes apparent that consent was overlooked, or was not genuine or informed. If the court has fulfilled its obligation to secure proper consent, this will not arise and it is also important to distinguish instances where the offender gave proper consent but is subsequently indicating unwillingness to comply with the order. Nevertheless, instances may very occasionally arise where the sentence could be reconsidered by the court in the light of the offender's indication that s/he did not give consent at all or gave it on an incorrect premise. This question should be taken up with their legal representative in the first instance and this may well help to resolve matters without the necessity of formal action. It is worth noting that the *National Standards* (1992 version) for probation and community service orders require that at the first meeting it should be established that informed consent has been given to the order, with the instruction:

> 'if not, and the offender states that he or she refuses or withdraws consent, take appropriate action, if necessary by returning the offender to court'.

The old *Standards* did not indicate by which legal device such a referral back to the court should be achieved but appeared to fudge the difference between instances where true consent has not been given, where variation would be justified, and those where consent properly given is now withdrawn, where breach or revocation action would seem the appropriate course. The 1994 version is silent on this issue.

• To increase sentence where the court feels that the original sentence was imposed on a factually incorrect basis. The reported cases illustrating this possibility concern instances where the offender had made claims in mitigation which caused the court to take a lenient view but which rapidly proved to be ill-founded. Thus in *R v Hart* (1983) 5 Cr App R(S) 25 a suspended prison sentence imposed on the strength of the offender's claim that he was going abroad with his girlfriend to start afresh was replaced with an immediate term when it came to light that this was untrue and had been invented simply to sway the court. Likewise, in *R v McLean* (1988) 10 Cr App R(S) 18, sentence of immediate custody was increased when the offender who had promised the judge that he was remorseful and intent on changing his ways promptly escaped from custody through an inadvertently open door. It is not difficult to think of instances where community sentences are imposed on the strength of good intention or mitigation which soon evaporates or proves to be groundless. However, unlike the position with custodial sentences, the court retains some oversight of the order and the opportunity to re-sentence in any subsequent breach or revocation proceedings (which are likely to follow in some instances of bogus assurances) and it would usually seem preferable for the court to exercise control by those means. Although the court certainly has the discretion to increase sentence when exercising variation powers, the Court of Appeal has indicated that this should be done only in exceptional circumstances which undermine the whole basis of the original sentence (per Woolf LJ in *McLean*).

• To impose a different form of sentence in the light of new information that becomes available to the court. Thus in *R v Sodhi* (1978) 66 Cr App R 260 a prison term was replaced by a hospital order in the light of psychiatric opinion that the offender was suffering from paranoid psychosis. Though it would seem unfortunate for a court to go ahead with sentencing when information of this important nature is pending, there may be rare instances where new information transforms the basis of judging the offender's suitability for a particular community sentence. This situation may, however, be dealt with more appropriately and flexibly, without worry of time limit, by revocation proceedings.

Procedure for Variation

There is no precisely defined procedure for bringing such exceptional instances to the court's attention. *Stone's Justices Manual* (1994, 1–2235) suggests that an application may be made by the offender or the prosecution or the court may, of its own motion, reconsider a sentence. Variation should take place in open court and the defendant or his legal representative should have an opportunity to address the court. In magistrates' courts the varying court should consist of the same magistrates who dealt with the case originally or at least the majority of that Bench (s 142(4)).

Outside the 28 day Period

A sentence may not be varied after the expiry of the 28 day limit. The matter will then have to be taken on appeal by the usual route either to the Crown Court or to the Court of Appeal. However, the Crown Court has an inherent jurisdiction, separate from its power under SCA 1981 s47(2), to remedy mistakes in its record and so corrections of a very minor, technical nature, not involving, for example, change in the length or requirement of an order, can be dealt with by exercise of that inherent jurisdiction.

Effect of New Sentence

MCA 1980 s142(5) specifies that the sentence or other order as varied shall take effect from the beginning of the day on which it was originally imposed or made, unless the court otherwise directs.

16.
REVIEW OF LENIENT SENTENCES

Usually, the prosecution has no right to challenge or appeal against a sentence which is considered to be too lenient. However, a limited exception was introduced by CJA 1988 ss 35 and 36 which gives the Attorney-General power to refer to the Court of Appeal cases in which it appears that the sentencing by the Crown Court has been 'unduly lenient'. Reference can only be made if:

(i) the offence for which sentence was passed is triable only on indictment, or is an 'either way' offence which the Home Secretary has specifically made subject to this procedure, and

(ii) the Court of Appeal gives leave.

So far, the power of reference has been extended to only three 'either way' offences, sentenced on or after 1 March 1994 (CJA 1988 (Review of Sentencing) Order 1994):

indecent assault on a male or female

cruelty to or neglect of children (CYPA 1933 s1)

making threats to kill.

The power does not apply where these offences are sentenced by a magistrates' court but does apply where the offender has been committed to the Crown Court for sentence. Notice of application for leave to refer a case must be given within 28 days from date of sentence.

When reviewing sentence upon the Attorney-General's reference, the Court of Appeal may quash the Crown Court's sentence and substitute any other sentence that the Crown Court has power to impose. The Court of Appeal has indicated that it will not intervene unless it is of the view that there was some error in principle in the judge's sentence, so that public confidence would be damaged if the sentence were not altered (*Attorney-General's Reference No. 5 of 1989* (1990) 90 Cr App R 358).

In reviewing sentence, the Court of Appeal should take account of the position as it now stands, including any indication of the offender's efforts since the original sentence was passed. Thus if a community sentence was imposed, the Court will be able to consider a report from the Probation Service about the offender's response to date.

Overturning a Community Sentence

Though the Court of Appeal is by no means confined in its discretion to increasing the Crown Court's sentence, this is a very likely outcome. Thus a community sentence imposed for a serious offence may well be challenged and overturned. *Attorney-General's Reference No. 27 of 1993* [1994] Crim LR 465 provides a recent illustration. On pleading guilty to causing grievous bodily harm with intent, for attacking an opposing player during an association football match, the offender had been sentenced to a probation order with a requirement of attending a 'violent offenders' programme'. The Court of Appeal understood 'that it might be in the best interests of the offender that he should be rehabilitated' but 'the idea that conduct involving an intention to do really serious bodily harm is to be dealt with by putting a person on probation should not be allowed to become current'. A period of imprisonment was substituted.

However, in exceptional circumstances, even where the Court of Appeal considers that the sentence was unduly lenient, discretion may be exercised to allow that sentence to stand. Thus in *Attorney-General's Reference No. 18 of 1993* [1994] Crim LR 467, a probation order with a requirement that the offender should receive treatment for alcohol dependency, imposed for GBH with intent (aiming a blow with an iron bar at a pregnant woman, instead hitting a small child on her knee), was allowed to continue. The Court took account of a letter from the child's mother asking that no further sentence be imposed and a report from the Probation Service that the offender had responded extremely well to the requirements of the order. Note also *Attorney-General's Reference No. 4 of 1989* [1990] 1 WLR 41 where the Court quashed a suspended sentence imposed for incest and replaced it with a three year probation order at a probation officer's suggestion, acknowledging that a custodial sentence would hamper the intensive therapeutic work being undertaken with the family by the Social Services Department.

APPENDIX: CASE ILLUSTRATIONS

1. Maurice Darncing: Probation/Supervision Order

Convicted of aggravated vehicle taking at the Crown Court sitting at Casterbridge, Maurice Darncing (aged 17) is sentenced to a probation order for two years. He is intending to move immediately after the court case to live with his father in Melchester and so the order specifies the Melchester petty sessions area. The order contains an additional requirement under PCCA 1973 sch 1A para. 3 that Maurice shall attend the Judge Jeffreys Probation Centre at Melchester for 60 days. Maurice duly moves to his father's home but after three weeks decides that the arrangement is not working and returns to live with his mother in Casterbridge, first informing his Melchester probation officer, Tessa Hardy, of his change of mind. He has not yet commenced the probation centre programme. Ms Hardy requests that Maurice reports weekly to the Casterbridge probation office to see the duty officer who subsequently confirms that he is reporting regularly and that his move back to Casterbridge appears to be permanent. There is no probation centre in or convenient for Casterbridge but Maurice is considered suitable for the 'End of the Road' programme, a motor project for young car offenders in Casterbridge, run by Social Services as a s12A(3)(a) specified activities requirement of a supervision order.

It appears clear that Maurice has changed residence from the Melchester PSA to that of Casterbridge and that jurisdiction should thus be transferred to that area. However, an application to the supervising court in Melchester (which in this instance, assuming that Maurice is still aged under 18, will be the youth court) cannot proceed straightforwardly under sch 2 para. 12(1) and (2) because the order contains a requirement which cannot be complied with unless Maurice continues to reside in Melchester. The court must first resolve that obstacle under the provisions of para. 12(3)(a) or (b) (see page 27). The court might opt to cancel the requirement of probation centre attendance but is perhaps unlikely to do this so soon in the life of a Crown Court order where that requirement was clearly integral to the judge's decision to make the order and has not yet been even partially complied with. The alternative is to delete the probation centre requirement and to substitute a further requirement which can be complied with in the new PSA. The obvious substitute requirement is to attend the Social Services 'End of the Road' programme. This could properly constitute a requirement in a probation order, despite being run by another agency, under PCCA 1973 sch 1A para. 2, probably under para. 2(1)(b) (requirement to participate in activities under the instruction of the person in charge for up to 60 days). However, to impose such a requirement requires the consent of the person whose co-operation is needed and it will need to be investigated whether the programme leader is willing to allow attendance to be a feature of a probation order instead of a supervision order.

If the leader is agreeable, the order will have to be amended under sch 2 para. 13(1)(b) (inserting in substitution for an existing requirement any requirement which could be included if the court were then making the order). This amendment cannot be made on the application of the supervising officer without attendance and consent of Maurice (para. 17(1)) who must be summonsed to appear before the court. This would require a fairly substantial (and expensive) journey by Maurice for what is likely to be a relatively brief and largely formal hearing. An alternative would be to invite Maurice (with the help of his Casterbridge probation officer) to make the application for the para. 13 amendment, in writing and expressing his willingness to comply with the 'End of the Road' requirement, to be presented by Ms Hardy at the same time as she seeks the para. 12 amendment. The court are not obliged to proceed on the basis of a written application but in the circumstances may well decide that it is appropriate to do so. If the court declines to deal with the application in this way, then Maurice's presence will be necessary, either to make application in person under para. 13 or to express consent to the new requirement on Ms Hardy's application. Either way, the court will be able to order the two amendments in tandem so that a new additional requirement, compatible with the new area of residence, is substituted, and Casterbridge PSA is substituted for Melchester PSA.

If Social Services decline to accept Maurice under the terms of a probation order (eg because they insist on a requirement of 90 days attendance as allowed under a supervision order), the challenge becomes more daunting. If the objective remains for Maurice to attend the 'End of the Road' programme as a requirement of statutory supervision, this will necessitate seeking revocation of the probation order so that Maurice can be dealt with afresh, this time by means of a supervision order with a s12A(3)(a) requirement. As the probation order was imposed by the Crown Court, revocation can only be ordered by that Court. If Ms Hardy makes application to the Melchester Youth Court, Maurice's attendance will be essential and this will be achieved by issue of summons. Maurice too may seek revocation and, as in the earlier amendment application, it might be worth asking the court to remit the matter to the Crown Court (sitting at Casterbridge) on the strength of Maurice's written application. However, given that the court has to commit him in custody or release him on bail pending the Crown Court hearing, the court will probably decline to proceed in his absence. Either way, assuming that the youth court considers that it would be in the interests of justice that the order should be revoked and Maurice should be dealt with in some other manner, the matter will be referred back to the Crown Court which will be empowered to revoke the probation order and to sentence Maurice to a supervision order with the 'End of the Road' project requirement. This is somewhat unusual in that it requires the replacement of an 'adult' disposal by a 'juvenile' measure but the court is at liberty to impose either form of statutory supervision on 16/17 year olds. Considerations of 'maturity' or 'stages of development' are not of statutory significance.

Note, however, that if Maurice attains age 18 prior to the revocation hearing at Crown Court the judge will not be able to impose a supervision order as he will no longer be of an eligible age as he must be dealt with 'as if he had just been convicted by the court'. If Maurice is very close to his 18th birthday at the time when the legal difficulties first become apparent, then it will not be worth embarking on the revocation route. Either some other form of programme or activity compatible with a probation order will need to be sought or, failing that, the Melchester court may have to face straightforward cancellation of the probation centre requirement, an amendment under para. 13 which does not require Maurice's attendance at court.

If Social Services agree to accept Maurice on the programme under the terms of a probation order but Maurice declines to consent to the substitution of requirement and the supervising court is reluctant simply to cancel the probation centre requirement, then the most appropriate course may be for the probation order to be referred back to the Crown Court with a view to revocation. This cannot be pursued on the supervising court's own initiative and would require an application for revocation either by Maurice or, more probably, by Ms Hardy as the responsible officer.

2.   Jon Harding: Probation Order

Convicted of several 'public order' offences including threatening behaviour, criminal damage, assaulting a police officer and being drunk and disorderly, Jon Harding was sentenced to a probation order for six months by Eastminster Magistrates' Court on 3 February. NFA at the time of his offences, he had been initially remanded to a bail hostel in Kingsborough but was subsequently remanded in custody when the bail bed was withdrawn following his breach of curfew. The pre-sentence report had suggested a conditional discharge, given the uncertainty of his future plans and his comparative lack of local ties, though his children by his previous marriage live in the Eastminster area. He remains NFA and the probation order specifies the Eastminster PSA.

Instructed at court to report to the Eastminster probation office duty officer on 9 February and to notify the office in the meantime if he obtained an address, Mr Harding called at the Fenbridge probation office on that date, stating that he was now seeking accommodation in that town but wanting financial help to travel to Kingsborough to fetch his belongings from the bail hostel. This request was refused but, on advice from the Eastminster office, he was told to report at Eastminster on 15 February. On 12 February he called at probation office No. 1 in Dockport, stating that he had been arrested in Kingsborough on warrant for non-payment of fines and brought to Dockport, a large urban area (200 miles from Eastminster) where hc has previously resided and still has family connections. He unsuccessfully sought a travel warrant to return to Eastminster but, on advice from Eastminster he was instructed to report to the Eastminster office on 15 February.

On 15 February he called at probation office No. 2 in Dockport, stating that he was still NFA but now intended to remain in that area, and asked if his probation order could be transferred to Dockport. On 25 February he called at Dockport offices Nos. 1 and 3, claiming still to be NFA and complaining that the probation service was doing nothing to assist him to obtain accommodation and employment. The probation officers who saw him considered that he was 'too clean and tidy' to be genuinely NFA and that 'he must have an address somewhere locally'. He said he had to return to Eastminster in early March for a court hearing concerning contact with his children and he was accordingly instructed to report to the Eastminster office on arrival.

On 8 March following various communications with Dockport, the supervising officer in Eastminster wrote to Dockport requesting that probation supervision be undertaken there with a view to early formal transfer of responsibility.

On 9 March Mr Harding reported to Dockport office No. 2 stating he would be travelling to Eastminster the following day and was told to report to his supervising officer on arrival. He duly did so, indicating that he would be returning to Dockport and remaining there. He was instructed to report at Dockport office No. 2 on arrival. On 2 April he called at Dockport office No. 3, stating he was still sleeping rough. He was told that he should maintain contact with Dockport office No. 2. In the light of this information, the Eastminster SPO wrote asking the SPO at Dockport office No. 2 to accept formal transfer of the order as quickly as possible. On 15 April, Mr Harding visited Dockport office No. 2 and was given an appointment with an accommodation officer at Dockport office No. 3.

On 22 April, the Eastminster SPO, having heard nothing from the Dockport No. 2 SPO, wrote indicating that an application would now be made to the Eastminster Magistrates' Court for a substitution of PSA. On 26 April, the SPO at Dockport replied saying that this was out of the question – 'Mr Harding would appear to be dictating the terms of his own order and I wonder whether breach action would not be more appropriate than transfer… This man cannot be given reporting instructions and refuses to supply an address'.

If we stop the clock at this point in this somewhat convoluted but nevertheless true tale, it is clear that we are in the sphere of messy reality rather than 'best practice' territory. The exasperation in Eastminster at the making of this probation order, contrary to the PSR advice, is understandable. The difficulties of seeking to oversee an order over a substantial distance where the supervising officer has never met the offender are also obvious. Nevertheless, it seems fair to characterise the process so far as a somewhat inept game of 'pass the legal parcel'. What is clearly missing is an arrangement whereby the Eastminster officer requests and authorises Dockport colleagues to issue clear and consistent reporting instructions on Eastminster's behalf and instructs Mr Harding via Dockport staff to accept Dockport's instructions as Eastminster's 'agent'.

It is perhaps to Mr Harding's credit that he has persevered, reporting on ten occasions during the first ten weeks of the order – in substantial compliance with *National Standard* expectations. The Eastminster SPO could have proceeded to seek unilaterally a substitution of PSA amendment, as the supervising court is not required to consider the view of the probation service in the new area, though this would in practice be considered extremely discourteous and poor form.

The Dockport SPO suggests that breach proceedings should be initiated but it is difficult to follow what grounds can be alleged. The belief that he must have a Dockport address but is refusing to notify this may be a well-grounded suspicion but on what basis could an allegation that he had failed to notify change of address be proved without evidence that he has an actual address? Failure to comply with reporting instructions would offer a much sounder basis for prosecution but the reluctance of any one Dockport office to assume de facto responsibility has meant that the offender has been largely obliged to 'dictate the terms of his order'. We can now resume the narrative.

On 26 April Mr Harding reported unexpectedly at the Eastminster office, still claiming to be NFA but stating that he now planned to remain in Eastminster. His supervising officer instructed him to report next on 4 May. Mr Harding did not do so and with evident relief the supervising officer immediately laid an information on oath alleging this failure to report and secured a warrant not backed for bail. Arrested on 15 May and still NFA, Mr Harding was bailed by a Saturday occasional court to appear at court on the following Monday. He answered to bail and entered a plea denying the breach allegation. It is clearly possible that an offender who is genuinely homeless may well be able to claim 'reasonable excuse' for non-attendance if their circumstances make other demands on their energies more pressing.

In this instance the clear, nay fervent, wish of the supervising officer was to use breach proceedings as a route to securing revocation of what was regarded as a totally unsatisfactory order. Prior to the hearing, the court duty officer had discussed the options with the duty solicitor and was aware that a denial would be made. It was pointed out that Mr Harding might make his own application for revocation of the order, as he was now stating that he was completely out of patience with the probation service, that his future plans were fluid and that he wished to cope with his problems unaided. Unable to consult the supervising officer or the SPO, the court duty officer made an on the spot judgement that such an application by the offender would not be opposed, and in fact gave an oral response, outlining the short history of the order and advising that the offender's circumstances and attitude made him unsuitable for statutory supervision. The court granted the offender's application and, on the court duty officer's indication that no evidence would be offered on the breach allegation, this was formally dismissed. The court then proceeded to deal with Mr Harding afresh, reading the original PSR, and imposed a conditional discharge, as indeed that report had proposed. This use of procedure may not accord fully with the Court of Appeal's indication that alleged breach misbehaviour should be put to proof (see page 55) but the outcome has pragmatic appeal as a convenient, inexpensive way of resolving the case reasonably fairly.

This case illustration should not be taken to imply that homeless or itinerant offenders are unsuitable for probation orders; a commitment to equal opportunities demands that flexible arrangements should be made to facilitate their compliance with the order compatibly with their mode of life.

3.   Sheila Peel: Community Service Order

A community service order for 150 hours was imposed on Ms Peel for burglary by the Crown Court at Lymeswold in October 1992. She was already subject to a probation order for two years imposed in July 1992 by Stilton Magistrates' Court. The order specified the Stilton PSA. Ms Peel is a single parent with two children aged six and four. At her initial interview she undertook to work each Monday.

Between October 1992 and March 1993 she worked on eight occasions, completing 69 hours, being excused attendance on a number of dates because of child care commitments such as children's illnesses and including the whole of the school Christmas holiday. After a number of failures to attend for work in April 1993, informations were laid alleging her failure to work as instructed on three dates and a summons was issued on 29 April for her to appear before Stilton Magistrates on 27 May. On her failure to appear on that date, a warrant was issued backed for bail to appear on 24 June. On that date she entered a denial of all three allegations and the case was adjourned to 15 July at the request of the defence who wished to obtain medical evidence to substantiate Ms Peel's claim of 'reasonable excuse'. The defence solicitor was also querying whether the order could be completed as Ms Peel was pregnant and expecting to give birth in October. On 15 July a trial date was set for 25 August, but this was later re-listed at the defence's request to 17 September, as medical evidence was still awaited. On 2 September Ms Peel gave birth prematurely.

At the expected trial on 17 September, the defence produced medical evidence indicating the problematic history of the pregnancy and other stress factors leading to depression and the relevant officer decided that the obvious course was to offer no evidence so that the breach allegations were dismissed. An application was made for the time period to be extended and, in the light of the recent birth and the baby's needs, an extension by 12 months was requested and granted. On 4 October Ms Peel's supervising probation officer requested that Ms Peel be excused attendance for CS work for four months to give her space to cope with the demands of her baby, including breast feeding the child.

At a meeting between Ms Peel, her probation officer and the relevant officer on 18 January 1994 to review the order, Ms Peel stated her wish to continue with the order, 81 hours remaining outstanding. She wished to arrange child minding and to hire a breast pump so that she could express milk for the child's feeds during her absence. She was given a list of registered child minders and informed that the relevant officer could arrange payment of both items of expenditure. She was instructed to report back to the relevant officer on 27 January so that she could confirm the arrangements made and be given fresh work instructions. As she failed to attend on that date, she was given a written instruction to come for interview on 1 February. She failed to attend on that date too and was sent further interview dates for 23 February, 4 March and 7 March all of which she failed to keep, despite warning letters. On 11 March informations were laid alleging that she failed to attend for interview on the latter four dates and a summons was issued for her attendance before Stilton Magistrates on 21 April. She failed to attend court on that date and a warrant was issued backed for bail to attend at court on 5 May. Appearing at court on that date she requested an adjournment to 19 May to obtain legal representation and stated that in view of various worries and strain she was experiencing in Stilton, she intended to move to stay for an extended period with her mother in London. She said that with her mother's help she would be able to resume CS work, if this could be arranged in London.

Appearing before the court on 19 May, she had not obtained legal representation and was still living in Stilton, with no immediate prospect of moving to London. She produced a note from her GP which outlined her parental responsibilities and her anxieties, including harassment by neighbours, but he admitted the four allegations of failure to comply. On the advice of the relevant officer, the matter was remitted back to the Crown Court at Lymeswold for the breach to be dealt with.

This enforcement exercise was clearly not a very satisfactory experience from any party's point of view. The offender clearly wished to avoid the jeopardy of re-sentencing at Crown Court yet had completed less than half of her order in 19 months and had not worked any hours for the past 13 months. If she had been breached on grounds of failure to work as instructed then she would almost certainly have been able to establish reasonable excuse but in this instance her failures to attend even for interview to discuss her circumstances appear to have left her with little option but to admit default. If she had attended for interview and explained her situation fully, the relevant officer may have opted to apply for revocation or have invited her to make such an application.